WRITING to 14

Geoff Barton

**Fiction Consultant:
David Almond,**
author of *Skellig*, winner of the
Carnegie Medal 1999

OXFORD

OXFORD
UNIVERSITY PRESS

Great Clarendon Street, Oxford OX2 6DP

Oxford University Press is a department of the University of Oxford.
It furthers the University's objective of excellence in research, scholarship,
and education by publishing worldwide in
Oxford New York
Athens Auckland Bangkok Bogotá Buenos Aires Calcutta
Cape Town Chennai Dar es Salaam Delhi Florence Hong Kong Istanbul
Karachi Kuala Lumpur Madrid Melbourne Mexico City Mumbai
Nairobi Paris São Paulo Singapore Taipei Tokyo Toronto Warsaw
with associated companies in Berlin Ibadan

Oxford is a registered trade mark of Oxford University Press
in the UK and in certain other countries

ISBN 0 19 831461 2

Typeset by Moondisks Ltd, Cambridge
Printed in Spain by Graficas Estella

Dedicated to my friend and colleague, Anne Forgham

Contents

Section 5: Personal writing

Section 6: Other non-fiction writing skills

Section 7: General fiction writing skills

Section 8: Character

Section 9: Setting

Section 10: Plot

Section 11: Writing style

Section 12: Extended writing

This book is designed to help you improve your writing skills. In school and beyond, you will be asked to write in a huge range of styles and formats – from History essays and accounts of Science investigations to stories, speeches and reports.

Writing to 14 aims to develop your writing in these and many more contexts. It helps you identify the essential skills, such as identifying your **audience**, clarifying the **purpose** of the writing and judging the appropriate **style**.

Audience is a key point. In the past a lot of writing in school had very little sense of audience. For example, here are some real essay titles set in exams in 1968:

Write two to three pages on one of the following subjects:	
	1 The most memorable evening's entertainment I have ever had.
	2 Give your views for or against the statement that 'the motor-car is now a curse rather than a blessing to mankind'.
	3 Describe an occasion when you missed the last bus or train.

Nowadays you are likely to get slightly more interesting topics and more guidance on how to approach the task. The Writing section of the KS3 English tests sets tasks like these:

1	Imagine you are a director of a new museum. (You can decide what is in the museum.) Write a letter to headteachers of schools in the area encouraging them to bring groups of pupils to visit the museum.
2	Write about a frightening encounter with an animal.
3	Imagine you have been given a chance to talk in a year assembly. Choose an issue you feel strongly about. Write your speech trying to persuade other people to support your views.

Notice how these questions are different from the 1968 examples. First, they follow two reading passages: a story about a class visiting a museum where the attendant puts a live snake around the teacher's neck; then a leaflet persuading people to change their opinions about wolves. You can see that the writing tasks build upon these reading activities.

But in addition, these newer questions ask you to think much more about the audience you are writing for, the purpose of your writing, and the form of writing you will use. All forms of writing – from letters and leaflets to dialogue and descriptive passages – have their own particular conventions of style, layout and language. If you know about these conventions, then writing in these forms becomes easier and more successful.

Writing to 14 is written to match the exact requirements of the tests you will sit in Year 9. More important, it is designed to support the range of writing you will be expected to do throughout secondary school.

I hope you will enjoy using it.

Geoff Barton

Writing to 14 is the latest in Oxford University Press's collection of skills books.

Writing skills have gained increased attention in recent years, in particular at Key Stages 1 and 2 with the National Literacy Strategy. This book aims to take these initiatives further, developing students' writing skills in fiction and non-fiction genres at KS3.

A systematic approach to writing skills

Writing to 14 is designed to improve the quality of students' writing by focusing much more specifically on the skills required. It is partly organized by genre, so that a student being asked to write, say, a fantasy story or leaflet can first become accustomed with some of the language conventions of these genres.

But the book also moves beyond genre into the more specific skills which students often struggle with and which we, as teachers, can easily take for granted. How to use quotations effectively, how to write a summary, how to build tension in your stories… these are the kinds of writing skills *Writing to 14* addresses head-on.

In keeping with the thrust of the National Literacy Strategy, the book is far more ambitious than we would have dared to be a few years ago. I now find myself teaching Year 7 students about point-of-view in fiction, something I don't think I formally encountered until I was an undergraduate.

As a result, we can expect the quality of students' writing to become much more precise and focused, more technically ambitious. My work with the students I teach has shown that careful structuring of activities in advance, making stylistic conventions of texts explicit, pays off in the quality of the finished assignment. *Writing to 14* is designed to make that process easier to manage in class.

One important point: this book treats writing as a craft, something which students of all ages and abilities can excel in. It isn't therefore stuffed with unattainable models that they are expected to aspire to. Too many of the guidelines I've encountered have said things like: 'Write the opening to an atmospheric story. Here's the beginning of *Bleak House* to get you started.'

That's disastrous, and goes against the spirit in which we want students' confidence and abilities to flourish. Therefore, whilst you'll find extracts from a range of writers, their work is not set up as a shrine to which students should tiptoe and genuflect. Instead, they are shown as craftspeople, people further on, perhaps, in the writing process than most of our students, but nevertheless writing real texts in the real world, from which students can learn practical lessons and skills to experiment with.

Organization

The book is written in double-page spreads. Each has a single central focus. Students are introduced to the skill and then taught it. The 'Writing Practice' section then encourages them to try the skill for themselves.

This is an important step. Each unit does not end with 'now write a leaflet or story'. That would be to miss the point. It focuses on the key skill taught within the unit and asks students to explore it for themselves. Sometimes they will be writing headlines, sometimes summarizing a text, sometimes converting a passage from one genre to another. The focus here is on small-scale manageable tasks designed to build confidence in the student, to internalize their understanding of the specific skill, so that they can then embark on more extended writing.

The final section of the book provides a range of extended writing opportunities – some of them as essential practice for the KS3 tests; others for working on in class and at home. These final activities should prove especially useful in all English Departments: they comprise self-contained extended units of work to be done over a series of lessons. I know from experience how useful this run of lessons can be, and how much students enjoy putting together an assignment which is tightly focused, easy to manage, and also rewarding to work on. I have therefore included three such activities, thinking that you might want to use one with each of Years 7, 8, and 9.

Each extended activity requires students to write in a range of genres and formats. They should refer back to the main body of the book to refresh their knowledge of the stylistic conventions and layout features of each genre.

Writing frames

The whole of *Writing to 14* is supported by a pack of photocopiable writing frames. These provide further guidance for students on how to get the content, layout and written style of their work right. Students whose linguistic range is smaller and who therefore need more scaffolding will find them especially useful. Activity sheets have also been provided, offering further practice in particular skills.

The symbol 1 on the page beside an activity gives the number of the writing frame or activity sheet which accompanies that activity.

Conclusion

This was a really enjoyable book to write – a synthesis of teaching writing in the classroom for the past fifteen years. I am especially grateful to David Almond, winner of the Carnegie Medal, for casting his eye over the fiction section. I can't think of anyone who has a more secure feel for what works and what doesn't.

I hope very much that you will enjoy using the book in your classroom and that, as a result, your students will become more excited and informed about the skills inherent in writing… leading to more ambitious, successful written work in a wider range of genres.

Geoff Barton
Suffolk
October 1999

Introduction

Whenever you begin a piece of writing, you need to think who your audience is. Your audience will affect the way you write and the topics you choose. For example:
- If you know your audience really well, you might write about **topics** you would not write about to strangers.
- If you hardly know your audience, you will probably use a more formal **style** than you would if writing to a best friend.

Changing your style to suit the audience is known as changing your **register**. Getting the register right means knowing:
- who you are addressing (your audience)
- how formal or informal you should be (tone).

Getting started

Imagine you have been asked to create a leaflet telling Year 6 children what life will be like in Year 7 when they arrive at your school.

What do you know about the **audience**?
- Their age (10/11)
- That they probably know something about the school, but probably not many details
- That they might be worried about moving to a new school.

How will this affect the **content**?
- You will want to keep the content positive – telling pupils what they'll be able to get involved in, how quickly they will find their way about, who they can ask for help.

How will this affect your written **style**?
- You will want to keep the language fairly simple (short sentences, familiar vocabulary) so that the pupils understand it easily.
- You will probably want to use a chatty, light-hearted tone to build the pupils' confidence.

Notice how thinking about the audience helps you to get the content and the style right.

Writing practice

1 Look at the grid below. Think about how you would make sure that your **style** and **content** suited the audience for each piece of writing.

Assignment	Who is your **audience**? Think about their age, their background, how much they will know already about the topic, and what they will be expecting from the text.	What sort of **content** will they be interested in?	What **style** of writing will appeal to them? (Simple or complex? Serious or light-hearted? With specialist words, informal terms, slang?)
Write a leaflet for senior citizens inviting them to a Christmas concert at your school			
Write a letter to a school friend in hospital giving all the gossip from school			
Write a horror story in the style of *Point Horror* novels			
Write a letter to your Headteacher complaining about school meals			
Write an email to a friend saying how awful school meals are			
Write an article to persuade people in your class to stop eating meat			

Introduction

For some written assignments, you will need to use formal language – but when?

It will depend partly on your subject and partly on your audience. If your audience is someone you know well (e.g. a friend), you will be more likely to write informally.

Some subjects demand a more formal tone – think of History, Geography and Science, for example. Here you are expected usually to write in an impersonal, formal way, stating information rather than giving too much of your own opinion.

Getting started

How do we show whether our language is formal or informal?

2

1 Choice of vocabulary

Some words are more formal than others.

a) Look at these words. They all have similar meanings. Place them in order of **most** to **least** formal.

mad	crazy	nutter	insane	loony	unhinged	bereft of reason

b) Choose three of the words below. For each one, try to think of three or more words with a similar meaning. Place them in order of **most** to **least** formal.

happy	big	enjoyable	nasty	fast

In your writing, beware of choosing complex words for their own sake. In general, keep vocabulary clear and direct. After all, you want your audience to understand your message.

2 Grammar

a) Formal language will often use more **formal structures**. Informal registers may not always use full sentences. They will also use elided verb forms ('won't' instead of 'will not').

Look the list of verb forms below and decide whether they belong to a formal or informal register:

> isn't   cannot   you've   she is   are not

b) Informal writing often uses **compound sentences** – clauses joined together with 'and', 'but' or 'or', like this:

> *This is our new car and we are very pleased with it but we think there may be a small problem with the radio and we'll have to get it checked.*

A more formal style might use **complex sentences**, like this:

> *Although the car is new, there seems to be a problem with it. The radio, which is proving unreliable, needs to be checked.*

Take this compound sentence and write it in a more formal style:

> *The computer wasn't working properly and we called an engineer but that didn't help and I can't print off my homework but it should be fixed soon.*

Writing practice

Here's the opening of an essay about *Macbeth*. At present the language is far too informal. Based on what you have learned in this unit, rewrite the essay so that the style is more formal.

> Macbeth is a really crazy guy. He's got loads of hang-ups. His wife's a bit of a nutter too. It all starts off on this heath and Macbeth meets three witches. They tell him he's going to be king and he starts to believe them and this is really the start of all his problems because up until this point he's been a really powerful soldier but now it all starts to go pear-shaped...

Informal language (and when to use it)

Introduction

For some written assignments, you will need to use informal language. If you are not sure, ask yourself the following questions:
- How well do you know the audience? (If you know them well, then it's probably all right to use an informal style.)
- Will the person be offended if the style is too informal?
- How much does the person know about the topic? (If they are really familiar with it, perhaps your style can be less formal.)

Once you're sure that you should write informally, you need to be confident about how to do so.

Getting started

How do we make written texts more informal?

1 Handwriting

Handwritten texts usually feel more informal. Compare these two letter openings:

Dear Mrs McDonald

Thank you for your recent letter. In response to your specific questions...

Dear Mrs McDonald
Thank you for your recent letter. In response to your specific questions...

2 Non-linguistic signs

Very informal texts may use symbols like kisses (xxxx) or emoticons (☺ ☹). They may also use more exclamation marks to express emotion:

Hi Pete!
Amazing news! Wait for it!! You'll never believe it but...

3 Grammar

Informal texts use more compound sentences, i.e. clauses joined together using 'and' and 'but'.

They use contracted verb forms – such as 'there'll' and 'we've'.

They sometimes leave out the subject of sentences, e.g. 'Got to go' (instead of 'I have go to go').

4   Vocabulary

Abbreviations often appear – such as 'v.' for 'very', 'Sat' for 'Saturday'.

Basic vocabulary is often used which would be avoided in more formal texts – e.g. 'nice', 'good', 'nasty'.

Informal vocabulary and slang terms are used – such as 'yuk!', 'yeah', 'hunk', 'cool'.

Writing practice

3 38 Based on all these ingredients of informal language, take the letter below and rewrite it to make it much more informal. Use handwriting, non-linguistic signs, grammar and vocabulary to change the register completely.

> Saturday 17 July
>
> Dear Ms Morris
>
> I hope this letter finds you well. Since I have not heard from you in a while I thought I would take the opportunity to drop you a line. I trust you are busy.
>
> I have very little news. I have only recently returned from my holiday at Disneyland Paris. It was extremely enjoyable. I stayed with my mother at a hotel on the outskirts of Paris and we commuted in daily by train. My favourite attraction was Indiana Jones and the Temple of Doom, although I found the queue distressingly long.
>
> I look forward to hearing your news.
>
> Alex

Planning an essay

Introduction

Sometimes in English you will be asked to write essays. These are pieces of writing which give an opinion or a response to a specific question. Look at these examples:

> - 'Human beings are destroying the environment'. Do you agree?
> - Read these two poems about animals and write a comparison of them.
> - Write a character study of Macbeth, showing how he develops during the play.

To write a good essay you need to:

1 Plan a clear structure.
2 Use interesting, varied language.
3 Give specific examples so that your essay doesn't feel too general.

This unit teaches you about planning; the next tells you about essay styles.

Getting started

Part of the secret of a good essay is careful planning – knowing in advance what you want to say.

In some essays the structure is easy to decide upon. Take the example from above:

> Write a character study of Macbeth, showing how he develops during the play.

Here the best structure would be to describe Macbeth at the start of the play, and then show how he changes and develops during four or five key points in the play. The structure would be **chronological** – following the order of events in the text.

But what if the essay title was, 'Write about reasons for and against keeping animals in captivity, rather than leaving them in the wild'? Here is a possible approach:

1 Start by brainstorming ideas. Make two lists of ideas – one of arguments FOR zoos and wildlife parks, the other of arguments AGAINST.
2 Think of specific examples you will be able to use to back up your ideas – zoos/wildlife parks you have been to or heard about.

3   Then think about your opening paragraph, one which will introduce the topic.
4   Then number the points you have made in your two-column list, so that you use the most important ideas first and then move onto the less significant ones. This stage is really important – it is where you plan the structure of the essay.
5   Finally, think about your conclusion: what you will say to sum up the essay. Aim to write three sentences, so that it does not feel too abrupt.

Here is an example of what your finished structure might look like:

1   Arguments for leaving animals in the wild:
   • That's where they belong
   • More natural
   • Keeps animals wild, rather than 'taming' them
2   Examples of where leaving animals in the wild is best
3   Arguments for zoos/wildlife parks:
   • Saves some animals from extinction
   • Allows humans to learn about animal behaviour
   • Zoos can be safer for animals – protects them from predators
4   Examples of zoos/wildlife parks which are really educational and help animals
5   Conclusion:
   • Zoos serve an important purpose
   • But small cages, etc., can remove an animal's dignity
   • My opinion – need to create better zoos, like safari parks, so that animals can remain wild and allow us to learn about them

Writing practice

4 5
6 7

Write an essay plan for one of these essay titles:
1   What are the reasons for and against giving up meat?
2   Many people say that more choice of television channels has led to lower standards of programmes. What is your opinion?
3   Thirty years ago, the first human being set foot on the moon. What are the arguments for and against continuing our exploration of space?

Making opinion essays interesting

Introduction

Like newspaper articles, good essays capture our attention from the beginning and make us want to keep reading. A good essay may have lively and interesting **content**, but it also needs to be written in an entertaining **style**.

The style you use for your essay will depend on your topic, purpose and audience. Take Science essays. You might write up an experiment by saying, 'First we tested the zinc by…' – your style will be clear and **personal** (you describe what **you** did). However, if you are writing about an idea or concept you might be more **impersonal**: 'Filtration removes solid particles suspended in a liquid when they are passed through a filter, usually porous paper, plastic or cloth.'

On the other hand, an English essay about things which go wrong during Science lessons will have a **personal**, **informal** style.

Writing that is intended to inform will often be less personal than writing which entertains and persuades.

In this section we are going to look at styles in English essays.

Getting started

Imagine that your assignment has this title:

> Many people say that more choice of television channels has led to lower standards of programmes. What is your opinion?

In an essay, your opening paragraph is all-important. You need to get your audience interested. Here are some possible techniques:

1 Dramatic opening sentences

These immediately grab the reader's attention with a statement that is dramatic or controversial:

> Most television is terrible. Most television is boring. Most television is pointless. So why are we so addicted to it?

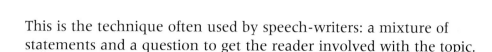
This is the technique often used by speech-writers: a mixture of statements and a question to get the reader involved with the topic.

2 Using quotations

If you can do some research using a dictionary of quotations, you might be able to find a quotation to kick your essay off – for example:

> *'Some television programmes are just so much chewing gum for the eyes.'*
> — John Mason Brown

You can build quotations into your style in several ways. The best is probably to allow the quotation to make an impact at the start of your essay, like this:

'Some television programmes are just so much chewing gum for the eyes,' said John Mason Brown. He sums up what many people think...

Style hint

Students used to be advised to keep their style very formal – never to say 'I' and 'me', and to avoid elisions like 'don't' and 'isn't'. For most English essays, these guidelines create a style which is too formal. The main ingredient should be you – your thoughts and feelings. Aim to write in a lively, interesting way, varying your sentences, choosing interesting vocabulary, and backing up your ideas with specific examples where you can.

Writing practice

SEE ALSO: Formal language (and when to use it) – page 12
Using quotations in literature essays – page 22
Using emotive language – page 44

Practise writing the opening of an essay using the techniques listed above. Choose one of the titles below.
1 Write about an event that made a big impact on your life.
2 Do you think the Internet has done more harm than good?
3 Write about a member of your family who has influenced you.

Writing openings for literature essays

Introduction

In literature one of the big dangers is writing a very general introduction, rather than getting to the heart of the question. This unit gives you advice on getting your essay started.

Getting started

A literature-based essay will need a less dramatic, more factual opening than an opinion-based essay. Try to go straight to the heart of the question, rather than re-telling the story or describing the writer's life.

Imagine this is your essay title:

> Write a character study of Macbeth, showing how he develops during the play.

Now compare these good and bad examples of opening sentences:

Good example:
At the start of the play Macbeth is a hero. People describe him as...

Bad example:
Shakespeare wrote his famous play Macbeth in 1601 and generations of theatre-goers have followed Macbeth's decline with fascination...

The good example immediately introduces the subject of the essay: Macbeth's character.

The bad example doesn't do this: instead, it begins with some general facts about the play *Macbeth* which have nothing to do with the essay title.

Look at exactly what the essay question is asking, and try to start addressing this directly in your first sentence. In examinations particularly, there simply is not time to make general points: you need to show the examiner that you know your stuff.

Here are some more examples:

Question 1	Compare Seamus Heaney's and Liz Lockhead's poems, saying which you prefer.

Opening sentence 1:	Seamus Heaney and Liz Lockhead both write descriptions of people. Heaney's poem is called 'Thatcher' and this abrupt title immediately tells us the occupation of the subject...

Notice:
- the opening sentence refers to both texts, to show that it is a comparative assignment
- the assignment then moves directly into an analysis of the first text
- the writer avoids a vague, general introduction
- the writer starts by focusing on the title of the poem.

Question 2	Write about the character of Sammy, showing how she develops through the play.

Opening sentence 2:	At the start of the play Sammy is immature...

8

Notice:
- the direct opening sentence
- the clear structure – we begin at the start of the play and will follow Sammy's progress through.

Writing practice

SEE ALSO: Thinking about audience and register – page 10 Formal language (and when to use it) – page 12

Think back to the last class text you studied – perhaps a novel, short story or play. Imagine that your assignment is to write an account of the main character in the text. Write an opening paragraph to your assignment which applies the techniques you have learnt in this unit.

Remember to:
- get straight to the point
- avoid a general introduction
- focus on the writer's language
- support points with quotations.

Using quotations in literature essays

Introduction

After writing the opening to your essay it will be vital to support your ideas with quotations.

Getting started

There are several rules to follow when using quotations:

1 Use the right punctuation

Punctuating quotations:
a reminder

1 Quotation marks go around the words a person says.

'Hail to thee, Thane of Cawdor,' says one of the witches when she sees Macbeth...

3 If you use 'said', 'replied', etc. after the quotation it has a small letter because it is part of the same sentence.

2 Quotations begin with a capital letter. They always have punctuation marks at the end – inside the quotation marks.

2 Get the layout of quotations right

If the quotation is less than a sentence long, place it within your own sentence; if it is more than a sentence (or more than a line of poetry) long, make it a paragraph on its own.

3 Keep quotations short

In general, keep quotations short. Using long quotations where they are not necessary can clog your essay up, making it slower to read because of the slabs of quotations it contains – like this:

Bad example:
We can tell that Hermia is sensitive about her height because she says:

Puppet? Why so - Ay, that way goes the game.
Now I perceive that she hath made compare
Between our statures...

A better approach is to pick out the key words you want and to embed them in your own sentence:

Good example:
We can tell that Hermia is sensitive about her height because she picks up on Helena's use of the word 'puppet'. Her strong feelings are shown when she describes herself in the same speech as 'so dwarfish' and 'so low'. This shows one reason for Hermia's jealousy of Helena…

Notice how much 'tighter' the essay feels – the short quotation gives it pace and allows the writer to make a point swiftly and precisely.

Writing practice

9 Take this extract from an essay and rewrite it so that the quotations are used more effectively by being embedded in the writer's sentences.

The opening scene shows us that the Duke is deeply in love. He uses dramatic vocabulary and seems obsessed with the sounds he hears:

If music be the food of love, play on;
Give me excess of it, that, surfeiting,
The appetite may sicken and so die.
That strain again! It had a dying fall…

To him, love seems like something you consume. It is interesting that he uses words related to death.

Writing a review

Introduction

During your English course you might be asked to write a review of a book or play you have seen, or even of a film. Reviews appear in newspapers every day. They have a double purpose: to inform readers (so that they know whether to read the book or see the film), but also to entertain them. The best reviews make us laugh, or think, or even make us feel angry.

There are usually two elements in a good review:

1   Factual: what the play/film is about or what the song/product is like, e.g.:

> '**T**his is the latest song by**…** taken from their last CD…'

2   Opinion: telling the reader how good it is, e.g.:

> Overall, this is a disappointment. The band seem to have lost their energy and many of the lyrics feel as if they were written on the back on an envelope during a lunchbreak. I had hoped…

Getting started

Think first about **structure**. You will probably want to give the fact-based information first before moving on to give an opinion.

You will also need to decide what you think of a performance or book. Once you have done this, you can spend time crafting your comments. Here are some examples of the creative way critics wrote about the movie *The Phantom Menace* when it opened in UK cinemas in July 1999:

All the actors are 'astonishingly bad. Neeson is on Mogadon*. He doesn't just phone in his performance, he puts it in the post without enough stamps on it.'

*Mogadon – a tranquillizing drug

Peter Bradshaw,
The Guardian

Watching the film is like going to visit an old friend who used to be the most entertaining person in the world, 'and slowly discovering they have become a bit of a bore'.
Cosmo Landesman,
The Sunday Times

By far the most irritating character is Jar Jar Binks, 'a wrist-flapping, deer-faced twit of an alien with the voice of a Jamaican drag queen'.
Robert Hughes,
The Independent

<u>McGregor</u>, playing the young Obi-Wan Kenobi, 'looks as if he just sat on the sharp end of a light-sabre'.
Anthony Lane,
The New Yorker

Notice how these comments work:
- visual images: 'wrist-flapping, deer-faced'
- similes: 'looks as if he just sat on the sharp end of a light-sabre'
- metaphors: 'Neeson is on Mogadon'.

Their tone is highly critical of the film, and yet designed to make us laugh.

Reviews don't have to be so unkind. They can also praise the qualities of a book, film or performance. Theatre and book critics, in particular, often use precise vocabulary to describe their responses. Here are comments on a new novel by Margaret Forster, *The Memory Box:*
- 'an interesting idea for a novel which never really catches fire' (Julia Flynn, *The Sunday Telegraph*)
- an 'enthralling novel, written with detail and precision. It is gripping and persuasive' (Pamela Norris, *The Literary Review*)

The secret here is to make your own vocabulary interesting and precise enough to give a strong flavour of what you are reviewing.

Writing practice

10 11

12

1 Choose something to review – a film or video, book or theatre performance, a meal out or the design of a new car or computer.
2 Plan a structure – the first part describing the product, text or performance, or summarizing the storyline (without giving too much away); the second part giving your opinion about it.
3 Experiment with the vocabulary, in particular finding synonyms for good or bad that will make your style more interesting, e.g.:

Some synonyms for good	lively enjoyable tense taut fascinating powerful evocative memorable amusing comic hilarious well-structured precise gripping enlightening entertaining convincing
Some synonyms for bad	dull tedious uninteresting uninspiring deadly banal unrealistic unconvincing depressing cliché'd slack unstructured rambling

SEE ALSO:
Formal language (and when to use it) – page 12
Writing a summary – page 62

Remember also the other techniques above – using visual images, similes and metaphors. Aim to write a review of around 200 words that informs *and* entertains.

Writing a biography

Introduction

How would you begin an article about someone else's life?

You might be tempted to start at the beginning – with details about where s/he was born and childhood days; or with the first major event in someone's life. This is the opening paragraph from an entry in the *Dictionary of 20th Century World Biography*. It is the beginning of a biography of Neil Armstrong, the first human to set foot on the moon:

> Armstrong entered Purdue University in 1947 as a naval air cadet to study aeronautical engineering but his course was interrupted by service in the Korean War, in which he flew seventy-eight combat missions and was shot down on one occasion. At the end of the war he completed his course…

1 How interesting do you find the article?
2 How much does it make you want to read on?

Getting started

Newspapers often feature biographies of people in the news. They sometimes call them profiles. The writers of these want readers to get hooked into the person's life-story from the first paragraph, so to start with their birth would be predictable and possibly boring. Instead, they use more dramatic techniques to capture our interest.

Here's how one journalist opens his profile of the astronaut Neil Armstrong:

> '**OK**,' said Buzz Aldrin. '*About ready to go down and get some moon rock*?'
>
> Thirty years ago, Neil Armstrong was preparing for the most momentous step made by a human being in the 20th century. But first he had to get there, wiggling his way out of the lunar module that had brought him and Aldrin this far. 'Forward and up; now you are clear. Little bit toward me,' Aldrin directed. 'Straight down. To your left a little bit. Plenty of room. OK, you're lined up nicely. Towards me a little bit, down. OK. Now you're clear. You're catching the first hinge,' he warned. 'The what?' asked Armstrong.
>   'All right,' said Aldrin. 'Move… To your… Roll to the left. OK. Now you're clear. You're lined up on the platform. Put your left foot to the right a little bit. OK. That's good. Roll left. Good.' Aldrin handed him a jettison bag: Armstrong would, among other tasks, take out the rubbish.

> 'OK. Houston, I'm on the porch,' said Armstrong. They adjusted the equipment, checking the sound and television picture.
>
> 'I'm at the foot of the ladder,' said Armstrong. 'The lunar module footpads are only depressed in the surface about one or two inches. Although the surface appears to be very, very fine-grained, as you get close to it, it's almost like a powder. Ground mass is very fine.' There was a pause. 'I'm going to step off the lunar module now.' There was a pause of several seconds before he spoke again as he swung his left foot down, the right still on the footpad, one hand grasping the module. 'That's one small step for man,' he said, 'one giant leap for mankind.'
>
> — Andrew Marshall

Notice how the writer:

- chooses one key moment from the person's life and uses this to grab the reader's attention
- uses detail (e.g. the surface of the moon) to help the reader see the scene
- uses dialogue to help bring the scene to life
- uses a formal style.

Writing practice

13

14

1   Work in pairs and interview someone in your class. Start by finding out the factual details about your partner's life (date and place of birth; parents; details of early years; family; early memories; nursery school; infant school… and so on).

2   Then talk to your partner about a significant moment in her/his life: for example moving house, changing schools, getting injured, losing a pet, getting lost, winning a competition. You will use this as the opening scene of your biography, so try to capture details about what it was like – the place; the atmosphere; what people were saying.

3   Then write a title: 'A Profile of [person's name]'. Use the key moment you have researched, and add detail and dialogue to bring the scene to life. Your aim is to capture the reader's interest in the person you are writing about, and to make us want to read on. Aim to write the first 150 words of a profile.

SEE ALSO: Formal language (and when to use it) – page 12

Writing a tabloid newspaper article

Introduction

Tabloid newspapers – like *The Sun, The Daily Mail, The Mirror, The Express, The Star* – are Britain's biggest-selling newspaper titles. Unlike broadsheet newspapers (such as *The Independent*), tabloids come in a smaller format which is easier to carry and read.

Because tabloid newspapers are aimed at a large audience, they tell their stories very directly. Here are some of the features of writing found in tabloid newspapers:

Writing feature	Effect
Large headlines and lots of pictures	Grabs our attention and makes us want to read
Plenty of stories about crime, showbusiness, royalty, scandals, arguments	Appeals to a wide audience and creates a feeling of excitement
Vocabulary that is easy to follow and not too complicated. Plenty of emotive words like 'cops', 'thugs', 'Brits', and dramatic words like 'Gotcha!' (used by *The Sun* in the Falklands War). Jokes and puns in the headlines	Ideal for a large audience who want to be entertained as well as informed by their newspaper
An opening sentence ('topic sentence') that tells the whole story. (Later parts of the story add more detail.)	Helps the reader to know quickly what the story is about
Short paragraphs – usually one sentence long	Gives a fast pace to the story
Lots of quotations from people involved in the story	Gives a strong human-interest dimension – people, rather than just ideas

Getting started

Here's the opening of a story from the BBC's website.

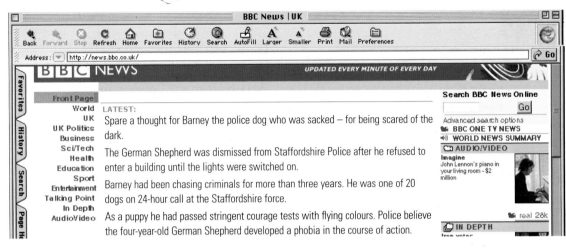

Now look at what happens when it is rewritten in the style of a tabloid newspaper:

IN THE DOGHOUSE

Barney the police dog has been hounded out of his job for being scared of the dark.

Four-year-old Barney had been one of Staffordshire's proudest pooches. Now he's on the doggy scrapheap.

Barney's terror of dark places was finally too much for bosses at police HQ and they ordered the German Shepherd to be put out to pasture.

Barney's trainer, Steve Doncaster, 32, said: 'It is a shame to let him go but we must consider the welfare of the dog and the safety of its handler.'

Writing practice

15

Use the notes below to make these points into a tabloid story:

- 14-year-old Stephen Fawcett of Wrexham, North Wales is well known at school for his animal impressions
- Hears smashing of glass at local library, phones police from call box, and then waits near library
- Thinks he sees thieves coming out from the broken window
- Does an impression of an Alsatian dog – the thieves go back in
- Police arrive and arrest them

1 Write a headline that will make readers want to read the story. In particular, brainstorm phrases and puns (word jokes) involving animals.

2 Write a topic sentence that tells the whole story.

3 Write the story in short paragraphs with lively, straightforward vocabulary.

SEE ALSO: Using quotations in newspaper articles – page 32

Writing a broadsheet newspaper article

Introduction

Broadsheet newspapers are sometimes referred to as 'the quality press'. They have a larger format than tabloid newspapers and go into more depth on many stories. They usually contain fewer stories about glamour, gossip and scandal, and give more space to topics like politics, economics and overseas news.

But we must not exaggerate the differences. Broadsheet newspapers are changing. Their readers often want detailed news coverage, but they also like human interest stories and being entertained.

Getting started

Compare these front page stories from tabloid and broadsheet newspapers on 25 July 1999. The headlines and first paragraphs show some of the differences in the two types of newspaper.

Broadsheet

Mortgage bosses face police probe

Bosses of some of Britain's biggest insurance companies could face criminal charges following a Scotland Yard investigation into alleged mis-selling of endowment mortgages.

The Sunday Times

Grants and loans chaos looms for all students

HUNDREDS of thousands of students are set to start the university year without their loan cheques because of huge delays with the Government's new student loan computer system.

The Independent on Sunday

Tabloid

SHE'S MY DOUBLE MIRACLE

PROUD mum in a MILLION Natalie Brown hugged her beautiful baby daughter Casey yesterday and said: 'She's my double miracle.'

The People

CRIMINAL

A **WOMAN** has been awarded £450,000 compensation after claiming a bungled hospital operation turned her into a criminal and wrecked her marriage.

The Sunday Mirror

Notice the differences:

Content
- Broadsheets focus on issues (finances, education, etc.).
- Tabloids focus on people.

Headlines
- Broadsheet headlines are longer.
- Tabloid headlines are snappier and more dramatic.
- Broadsheet and tabloid newspaper headlines both use typical newspaper words like 'probe' and 'looms'.

Style
- Broadsheets use more complex words – 'alleged', 'endowment'.
- They tend to use longer, more complex sentences and a more formal style.
- Tabloids use simpler, more emotive words like 'proud' and 'wrecked' and a more informal, colloquial (chatty) style.
- They tend to use shorter, simpler sentences.

Structure
Both types of newspaper structure their stories in a similar way:
1. Headline
2. Topic sentence telling the whole story
3. More details about the story
4. Quotations from people involved.

Writing practice

16 Make the following notes into a story for a broadsheet newspaper.

- Professor Jane Morris, Batley University, Yorkshire says schools are letting down pupils.
- They should teach more basics and cut out anything else for first six years – i.e. no PE, no Geography, History or RE, just English, Maths and Science.
- She says: 'This would provide a far better foundation for success than the current mixed diet of learning.'

- Government spokesperson says: 'The curriculum is always under review, but we would be unwilling to create anything quite as narrow as this.'
- Educationist Don Bousted says: 'I am appalled that anyone would suggest this. School should be about more than just learning basics. It is where children learn a whole range of skills. To scrap these would be a disaster.'

SEE ALSO: Using quotations in newspaper articles – page 32

Think of a headline – no more than seven words long.
Think of a topic sentence which summarizes the whole story.
Write the story in short paragraphs, using the style checklist from above.

Using quotations in newspaper articles

Introduction

Writers of newspaper stories usually aim to make the reader feel involved in the events they are describing. They want us to imagine what it must have been like to be there at the explosion, debate, disaster, concert, or other newsworthy event that they are covering.

One way of doing this is by using quotations, the words of people who took part in the story. Quotations can make a story feel more real, more believable, and add detail. They bring in a human-interest angle, showing us what people felt.

Getting started

In newspapers, the quotations are there to give the views of eyewitnesses. Here is an example of a newspaper report which uses quotations. The story has been edited to give you the first one or two paragraphs followed by the paragraphs containing the quotations:

A SCHOOL sports day was ruined when a family of seagulls viciously dive-bombed children and parents.

The screeching birds swooped from the roof at the front of the school where they kept patrol over their fully-grown chicks. School secretary Sally Watts said: 'We would not let the children go near the gulls. People had to run for cover and parents waiting by their cars were dive-bombed by the birds.

'When we had a disco in the evening we had to bring children in through a back lane. It was almost like a Hitchcock film. We have no idea where the gulls came from.

'When we rang the RSPB, they said the birds could not be removed because they are protected and suggested we should use umbrellas for protection.'

RSPB spokesman Graham Madge said yesterday: 'It's very rare for seagulls to affect a school like this and it's a very difficult position, legally.'

The Star, online edition, 20 July 1999

Notice how the writer has used quotations in this news story:
1 First, opening paragraphs set the scene by giving readers the whole story – who, where, what, when?
2 Then quotations help us to see what eyewitnesses saw.
3 The name of the person comes first, followed by 'said…' and the quotation. (But sometimes, the words a person says come first, followed by 'said…' or 'commented…')

4 Brief details of the speaker are often included: labels – 'RSPB spokesman Graham Madge' and, sometimes, age ('English teacher Jonathan Sharp, 34, said…'). (Occasionally anonymous witnesses are used – an 'insider', a 'spokesman'.)

5 The spokesman at the end of the story gives the story a sense of balance by showing a different viewpoint.

Writing practice

17 Here is the opening and ending of a real story from July 1999, plus some panels of bullet-point comments. Create the full story by building the bullet-points into quotations within the story. Look again at the list of techniques used by the newspaper writer in the example opposite.

Star Wars sets UK record

The Phantom Menace: Breaking box office records in the UK

Star Wars: Episode 1 – The Phantom Menace has broken UK box office records, raking in $15.1m (£9.5m) in its first four days.

The previous record holder in Britain was *Independence Day*, another sci-fi blockbuster, which took £6.9m ($10.8m) in July 1996 over its first weekend.

The Phantom Menace opened in the UK on 15 July. And despite the weekend of glorious weather that followed, thousands of eager fans found the lure of George Lucas's long-awaited Star Wars prequel too great to stay outdoors.

There were huge queues outside cinemas on the opening Thursday and they continued throughout the weekend.

Spokesperson for Warner Cinemas:
- 60,000 people on the first day
- 35,000 so far today

Fan, Saskia Macey (12):
- Seen it twice
- Thinks it's brilliant
- Hopes to see it again next weekend

Film Critic Leonard Vaux:
- Not surprised at success
- Lots of hype on television
- People are carried away – just as they were by the publicity for Titanic
- Big audiences don't mean it's a great film

BBC News online, 20 July 1999

Introduction

Newspaper **headlines** are designed to attract the reader's attention. Sometimes they use dramatic or emotional words, such as:

crisis	drama	clash	fury	battle	row

Slogans are the phrases used in advertising to help us remember a product. Here are some of the slogans used to advertise Coca-Cola over the past 20 years:

Coke is it!

It's the real thing

Have a Coke and a Smile

Always Coca-Cola

Headlines and slogans also sometimes use different kinds of wordplay – such as rhymes, alliteration and puns – to catch our interest.

Getting started

Start by learning about the techniques used in headlines and slogans:

Alliteration is the repetition of the sounds at the start of words. We are used to seeing it in advertising ('Pick up a Penguin'), but it is also a popular technique in newspaper headlines, e.g. 'New Bosnia Mercy Mission'.

Puns are jokes which use unexpected words – for example, imagine an American hen that escapes from a factory farm. Headline: 'Kentucky Freed Chicken'.

Rhymes and **half-rhymes** (also called assonance) are also used in headlines and slogans. Compare these two examples:

Full rhyme: 'St Helen's Glass has the Class' (full rhyme of 'glass' and 'class')

Half-rhyme: 'Beanz Meanz Heinz' (half-rhyme of 'Meanz' and 'Heinz')

Look at these headlines and slogans taken from an issue of A-Magazine, the magazine of Anglia Railways:

Subject	Headline/Slogan	Technique
Article about a successful fan-making company	Air of success	Pun
Article on enjoyable salads	Lettuce, pray	Pun
Article about garden design	The bold and the beautiful	Alliteration
Advertisement for Potmania	Norfolk's premier pot shop	Alliteration and half-rhyme
Article about safety in cars	Testing times	Alliteration
Article on mountain bikes	Blazing saddles	Pun

Occasionally, newspaper headlines can be confusing because they include accidental puns. Look at these examples. See if you can work out why they have double meanings:

New Jersey Judge to Rule on Nude Beach

Kids Make Nutritious Snacks

IRAQI HEAD SEEKS ARMS

STOLEN PAINTING FOUND BY TREE

Writing practice

18 Choose one of the scenarios below and think up some possible headlines or slogans. Try to use a range of techniques – such as alliteration, puns, full and half-rhyme.

Headlines *Try to think of headlines to make readers want to read these stories:*	Slogans *Try to think of slogans to make people want to buy these products:*
High exam results at your school	New low-sugar high-caffeine soft drink
A huge storm over your town	New watch, in which you can change the colour of its display
A footballer's shorts fall down during an important game	Supermarket claims lowest prices and fastest queues

For each of your ideas, label the techniques you have used.

Writing a feature article

Introduction

Feature articles are not written to report the news, although they may be topical, providing the background to news stories, profiles of people in the news or obituaries of people who have died. Other subjects for feature articles include music, gardening, fashion, opinion pieces, lifestyle journalism (about events, trends, the writer's own observations), and so on.

The subject-matter and the writer's style will depend on who the audience is, and everything must work to make the feature interesting for a reader.

Getting started

There are a number of ways to make your feature article interesting, as these openings from features journalism show:

1 Start with a human-interest dimension using a specific person

If you're asked to describe a large event – such as a riot in Los Angeles – you might begin by focusing on one individual:

> In front of the smoking electronics store, the small black boy had a problem. He had looted six items, but he could carry only five. For around fifteen minutes he hesitated, shielding them from other, older pillagers, while he tried to arrange them. Then flames spouted from the shop, driving out the remaining looters.
>
> *The Economist*

2 Start with a quotation

If you're asked to write about the creator of the Teletubbies, you might begin:

> **'I'VE HAD** white hair for a long time now,' Anne Wood considers between sips of gin and tonic. 'It's been a great advantage to me in the past: people underestimated me because of it, I'm quite sure. That's not as true now, sadly.' She stares off into the middle-distance for a moment as if genuinely sorry about this.
>
> *The Scotsman*, 20th July 1999

3 Pay close attention to visual detail: help your reader to see the scene

If you're writing about life on the streets of Paris, you might begin:

> **The rue du Coq d'Or, Paris, seven in the morning**. A succession of furious, choking yells from the street. Madame Monce, who kept the little hotel opposite mine, had come out on to the pavement to address a lodger on the third floor. Her bare feet were stuck into sabots* and her grey hair was streaming down.
>
> * sabots – wooden clogs
>
> — George Orwell

Notice how these writers aim to grab our interest, even if writing about topics that may not, on the surface, interest us.

Writing practice

19 20

21 22

Choose one of the topics below and write the opening 150 words of a feature article about it for a school magazine. The challenge is to make these topics interesting, so that the reader wants to read on. Experiment with the techniques above. Remember to:

- Think carefully about your audience. What will they be interested in? What will they already know about the subject? What style will you use?
- Spend time researching the topic – so that you can include visual details and quotations.
- Think about your opening sentence – you need to hook your reader's interest straight away.
- Use language in a way that will make the reader want to read on. For example, use vivid vocabulary that helps the reader to see the scene you describe.

SEE ALSO: Formal language (and when to use it) – page 12 Writing a biography – page 26

Topics:
1. A school event – for example, sports day or a concert
2. A description of a hobby or activity – for example, skiing or skateboarding
3. A profile of someone doing a particular job.

Writing a report 1 – factual reports

Introduction

A report is a factual piece of writing, written from first-hand experience. You could be asked to write a report about a large range of topics:

- a sporting event
- an accident
- a description of a meeting you attended
- an account of something that happened to you.

You might also be asked to write a report which is an evaluation – for example, judging which is the best make of video camera.

On this spread and the next, you are going to look at two different types of reports: reports which are purely factual – for instance, reports of scientific experiments – and other types of reports, which aim to entertain as well as inform.

Getting started

Scientific reports describe how things work or give an account of a science investigation. Your style will usually be factual, describing what you did, giving results, and then drawing conclusions. In the past students were sometimes taught to write in a very impersonal style, never saying 'I' or 'me'. Now, most reports contain a personal element, but the aim is still to keep the tone informative and factual.

Here's part of an example from a Year 8 student:

Aim

Our investigation was designed to find out which type of antacid tablet is most effective. We tested this by taking three different types of tablet, placing them all in water, and then adding acid to each one. This would show which tablet was most successful in neutralizing the acid.

Method

The three antacid tablets we tested were Rennie, Tums and Settlers. We placed each into 50 ml of water and allowed them to dissolve. We added methyl orange indicator to each one so that we would be able to see the effect of the acid. We then put 50 ml of hydrochloric acid into a measuring cylinder and slowly added this acid to each of the solutions, until the indicator changed colour. We wrote down how much acid had been added.

Results

Antacid	Volume of acid neutralized (ml)
Rennie	40ml
Tums	14ml
Settlers	23ml

Conclusion

Our investigation showed that Rennie was the most effective antacid – one tablet neutralized much more acid than the other two tablets. This means it would have much more effect in our stomachs, which also contain hydrochloric acid.

Science report style check

1   **Purpose:** to inform.
2   **Audience:** probably already knows something about the subject.
3   **Structure:** topic sentence starts with the aim of the investigation. Later parts of the report are chronological – describing how the investigation developed from start to finish. The final part is a conclusion, explaining the results and mentioning any problems.
4   **Style:** short sentences create a factual tone.
5   **Vocabulary:** factual – names of chemicals, equipment, quantities, and statistics. Some use of 'we' and 'I'. Other background details left out. (e.g. You wouldn't say: 'We did the investigation in the lesson before lunch. Miss Neal was wearing a crisp lab coat.')
6   **Other features:** charts and statistics to help communicate the information to the reader.

23

Writing practice

24

A police witness statement also needs to be very factual. Imagine that you saw a burglary taking place. Use the notes below to create a report for the police. Look back at the style check above, and make sure that you get the tone right.

SEE ALSO: Formal language (and when to use it) – page 12

- 7.45 yesterday morning – you were doing paper-round
- heard crash of glass at 34 Manor Garth
- then nothing – then man in blue T-shirt running with video
- dark hair – in his twenties – jeans – white trainers
- ran down drive, along passage to playing field
- you ran to 37, knocked on door and asked them to phone police

Writing a report 2 – reports which entertain

Introduction

A report of an event or incident may be designed to entertain as well as inform, depending on whom it is aimed at.

In class, you might be expected to write a report on:
• a visit – for example, a school trip
• an event – for example, a play you went to see
• a project – something you have worked on over a period of time (for example, writing up a drama performance you have been putting together)
• an investigation – the results of something you have been studying (for example, a review of student attitudes to school uniform).

Some of these will have a more personal tone than others.

The first three types of report – on a trip, an event, or a project – will all use a chronological structure – telling events in the order they happened. This means that the report may contain elements of storytelling as well as factual writing. You might use discourse markers like these: 'at first…', 'later…', 'then…', 'next…'. These all help the reader to see how you are structuring your ideas.

A report of an investigation may use a chronological structure if it includes an explanation of what you did during the investigation (i.e. the procedure), but it will probably use more facts and statistics than the other types of report.

Getting started

Here's an example from a Year 7 student:

A report on my visit to the National Railway Museum, York

We arrived at the Museum half an hour later than expected because of heavy traffic. We had to queue for a few minutes to collect our tickets. Then we walked through into the 'Great Hall'. At the centre of this is a huge turntable carrying a large locomotive called The Duchess of Hamilton. At angles from the turntable are a variety of other trains – large locomotives from around the world. From here we walked down some steps and underneath a train, so that you could look up to see how the mechanics of the wheels worked.

There is an exhibition of railway photographs, which includes a clever interactive display. You step into a large camera. Then, when someone outside stands on the special spot, it takes an instant photograph, projected onto a large screen inside the camera. It shows how cameras work.

Report style check

1 **Purpose:** chiefly to inform.
2 **Audience:** probably don't know about the place/event you describe.
3 **Structure:** chronological (starting at the moment you arrive; finishing when you leave). It might have a summarizing final sentence (e.g. why I enjoyed / didn't enjoy the day).
4 **Vocabulary:** factual, plenty of detail.
5 **Other features:** pronouns 'I' and 'we' show that this is a personal account.

Writing practice

25 Imagine that you have been asked to write a report on student attitudes to school uniform. Your report will be used by your Headteacher to consider small changes to the current code of dress.

Your report should include:
• an introduction, explaining what you aim to achieve and how you are approaching the task
• comments of students
• a summary of results (what the main findings are)
• conclusion – making a recommendation to the Headteacher.

A good report will contain:
• subheadings, to give it clarity
• evidence / facts / statistics
• a clear, easy-to-read style, which may use bullet-points as well as full sentences.

SEE ALSO: Formal language (and when to use it) – page 12

Keep your style fairly formal, but not pompous. In general, you will probably want to avoid using the pronouns 'I' and 'me' because the survey is not about your personal opinion.

Persuasive language in advertising

Introduction

Advertising language hates to be ignored. Whether it's in high-budget television commercials or small ads in newspapers, the aim of advertisers' language is to get a product or service noticed. An advertiser wants to persuade us that her or his product is the best available, so the language of advertising is often quite exaggerated. It's also often quite familiar – using clichés (well-worn words and phrases).

Getting started

Vocabulary

The language of advertising is often dramatic. Look at the following examples:

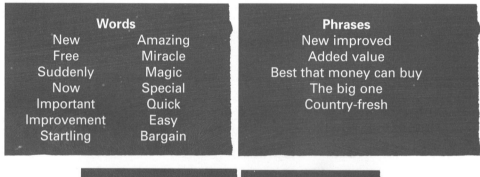

Words		Phrases
New	Amazing	New improved
Free	Miracle	Added value
Suddenly	Magic	Best that money can buy
Now	Special	The big one
Important	Quick	Country-fresh
Improvement	Easy	
Startling	Bargain	

Comparatives	Superlatives
Faster	Fastest
Better	Best
Happier	Happiest
Brighter	Brightest
More	Most

Grammar

Advertisements often use questions and imperatives (orders):

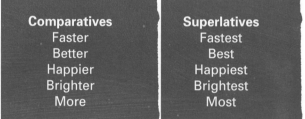

Questions	Imperatives
What's so different about our music?	Try it today.
Why is everyone talking about Hit-97FM?	Go on – change the way you look.

Writing practice

26

Now look at this example of a really bad magazine advertisement. It is supposed to be persuading readers to buy a new healthy breakfast cereal, aimed at 15-25 year olds. How would you change it to make it more eye-catching and dramatic?

You could:
- change the slogan
- change any words in the main text
- change the sentence types
- make suggestions for improving the design.

SEE ALSO: Using wordplay in headlines and slogans – page 34

Eat Kickstarters for Breakfast

Kickstarters are a really nice start to the day. They combine good flavour and healthy ingredients to make a very positive start.

You only have to add milk and Kickstarters are ready to kick you into gear. Kickstarters.

Why not think about trying out Kickstarters and see what you think of them?

Using emotive language

Introduction

Some writing assignments will test your ability to **persuade** your audience. One important technique is using emotive words.

Emotive words create an emotional reaction in the audience, as these two lists show:

Neutral words	Emotive words
tree car glass nicotine farm	anger agony hope shocking fury imprisoned freedom escape

Imagine how useful emotive words can be in writing persuasive texts. For example, you might be asked to write a leaflet aimed at young people, persuading them not to smoke; or a poster about the cruelty of factory farming methods.

Emotive words help you to get the reader really involved in a topic.

Compare these two examples about smoking:

Smoking is not good for you.

Smoking is not good for you. Cigarettes contain nicotine and this hurts your lungs very badly. The smoke is not good for you either. It can even dry up your skin so that by the time you are thirty you have started to look much older. Smoking can lead to very serious diseases.

People who are hooked on cigarettes forget some things. They forget the foul smells in their clothes, hair and teeth. They forget the way the smoke creeps silently into their skin, drying it out from the inside. They ignore the agony that disease will bring to them and their family.

Look at the way the second example grabs your attention. It uses repetition ('They forget… they forget… they ignore…') to create a rhythm, and it also uses **emotive words** to give the message more power.

Getting started

Explore emotive words more. Look at the word bank on the next page.
- How many of the words do you think are emotive (i.e. they create an emotional effect)?
- Which ones?

Compare your responses with a friend's.

| window | rage | sky | shattering | ink | job | gate | panic | desire |
| holiday | time | burning | sleep | | | | | |

Writing practice

27

Now use this writing frame to produce a leaflet. As you write, try to create an impact on your audience by using more emotive words.

Purpose: to persuade readers to give up eating meat
Audience: young people aged 11-16
Format: leaflet

Headline here – use an emotive word to grab the reader's attention (for example, 'murder', 'slaughter', 'cruelty', 'barbaric', 'terror', 'agony'…).

Give some information about meat-eating / how animals are caged. You might use bullet-points.

Now show what's in it for the reader in giving up – what s/he will gain. This time use positive emotive words, such as 'healthy', 'freedom', 'pride'.

XXXXXXXXXXX
Yyyyyyyyyy?

Mnmmnmnmn mnm
nmnm nmnm nmnm
nmn mnmn mnmn mnm
nmn mnm nmn
mn mnm nm
nmn mn
mnm n nmn
mnmn mnmn

Nnnnn

Mnmmnmnmn mnm
nmnm nmnm nmnm
nmn mnmn mnmn mnm
nmn mnm nmn

XXXXXXXXX

Subheading: use a question to get the reader involved: Why do you…? Have you ever questioned…?

Image: decide what image you would place here – something to grab the reader's attention.

Subheading: a word or two to keep the reader interested.

End with a slogan – a sentence or phrase that will stick in the reader's mind.

You could write about another topic if you prefer. Remember that the emphasis should be on using language that will create an emotional impact on your reader – emotive language.

Introduction

Leaflets used to be produced only by professional writers and designers. Home computers have changed that, and it is now fairly simple for anyone to produce an eye-catching message.

GUIDED CYCLE TOURS

To make the most of your time in Cambridge why not join one of our Leisurely Guided Cycle Rides. This is a unique and memorable way to see Cambridge. We will take you along the quietest cycle routes, in and around Cambridge, tell you about the places of interest and take care of any problems you might have with your bike. Our programme of guided cycle rides is aimed at occasional cyclists. Keen cyclists are still welcome, but will have to go at our leisurely pace. Geoff the guide and mechanic on these rides, is a Cambridge graduate who has a keen interest in local history and has been running a cycle hire business for 20 years.

TOUR INFORMATION

From April to September our Guided Cycle Tours around the Cambridge colleges normally run on Tuesdays, Wednesdays & Thursdays, at 2pm and on Saturdays at 10am. These tours take about 2 1/2 hours and cost £9.50 including bike hire. We will try to arrange tours at other times if required.

Please telephone Geoff on (01223) 365629 to book.

Remember, though, that leaflets are not just about design. They also depend on language which is well-judged for the audience. The language of leaflets and brochures is usually intended to make people notice the message quickly – there is no space for wasted words.

BIKE HIRE

Hire Charges June - August 1999

3 hours	£4.50	1 week	£15.00
1 day	£7.00	2 weeks	£25.00
2 days	£10.00	3 weeks	£33.00
3 days	£12.00	4 weeks	£40.00

Reduced rates for longer periods and in winter The hire charge must be paid in advance. In addition, a £25.00 deposit must be paid, fully refundable on safe return of bicycle. These prices are for our standard 3-speed or single speed hire bike, which are quite sufficient for getting around Cambridge.

Bikes with more gears are available at higher charges.

If you are hiring one of our bikes or have your own you are welcome to join one of our guided cycle tours at a reduced rate.

Visiting Cambridge for the day?

Then you will need a bike to get around the colleges and along the river.

Staying in Cambridge for longer?

Then a bike is an ideal way to get out into the surrounding countryside.

Studying in Cambridge?

Then join the local students cycling to school or college.

Come to Geoff's Bike hire where a large selection of bikes are available for hire at only £4.50 for 3 hours, or £7.00 for a day. All hire bikes come complete with basket and lock. They are also fitted with lights for those wishing to retain the bike overnight.

Cycling is for the whole family

All sizes of bikes are available for hire, and for those too small to pedal themselves there are bikes fitted with child seats. Trailerbikes and child trailers are also available.

Getting started

Leaflets are aimed at a clear audience. As a writer of these texts, you can't afford to waffle because you haven't much space. Look, for example, at the leaflet for cycle rides in Cambridge. Think about:

- the layout
- the intended audience
- the writer's style.

Notice:

- how the **layout** gives background information on the top left; facts on the bottom left and right
- How the **images**
  a) show attractive historical locations
  b) emphasize that this activity is safe for a family
  c) show an image of a clean-looking bike. These images are designed to be reassuring and attractive to potential customers.
- how the leaflet targets the **audience** directly – 'aimed at occasional cyclists', referring to them as 'you'
- how the writer's **style** reminds us of advertising language – for example using adjectives like 'unique' and 'memorable'.

GUIDED CYCLE TOURS

To make the most of your time in Cambridge why not join one of our Leisurely Guided Cycle Rides. This is a unique and memorable way to see Cambridge. We will take you along the quietest cycle routes, in and around Cambridge, tell you about the places of interest and take care of any problems you might have with your bike. Our programme of guided cycle rides is aimed at occasional cyclists. Keen cyclists are still welcome, but will have to go at our leisurely pace. Geoff the guide and mechanic on these rides, is a Cambridge graduate who has a keen interest in local history and has been running a cycle hire business for 20 years.

TOUR INFORMATION

From April to September our Guided Cycle Tours around the Cambridge colleges normally run on Tuesdays, Wednesdays & Thursdays, at 2pm and on Saturdays at 10am. These tours take about 2 1⁄2 hours and cost £9.50 including bike hire. We will try to arrange tours at other times if required.

Please telephone Geoff on (01223) 365629 to book.

BIKE HIRE

Hire Charges June - August 1999

3 hours	£4.50	1 week	£15.00
1 day	£7.00	2 weeks	£25.00
2 days	£10.00	3 weeks	£33.00
3 days	£12.00	4 weeks	£40.00

Reduced rates for longer periods and in winter. The hire charge must be paid in advance. In addition, a £25.00 deposit must be paid, fully refundable on safe return of bicycle. These prices are for our standard 3-speed or single speed hire bike, which are quite sufficient for getting around Cambridge.

Bikes with more gears are available at higher charges.

If you are hiring one of our bikes or have your own you are welcome to join one of our guided cycle tours at a reduced rate.

Visiting Cambridge for the day?
Then you will need a bike to get around the colleges and along the river.

Staying in Cambridge for longer?
Then a bike is an ideal way to get out into the surrounding countryside.

Studying in Cambridge?
Then join the local students cycling to school or college.

Come to Geoff's Bike hire where a large selection of bikes are available for hire at only £4.50 for 3 hours, or £7.00 for a day. All hire bikes come complete with basket and lock. They are also fitted with lights for those wishing to retain the bike overnight.

Cycling is for the whole family
All sizes of bikes are available for hire, and for those too small to pedal themselves there are bikes fitted with child seats. Trailerbikes and child trailers are also available.

Writing practice

28 29

Create your own one-side leaflet. Choose one of the topics listed.
Aim to make your leaflet as informative as possible.

Don't worry about drawing illustrations: just decide what image you
will put where, and label each space with a short description of its
image (just two or three words).

SEE ALSO:
Thinking
about audience
and register –
page 10
Using word-
play in
headlines and
slogans –
page 34
Persuasive
language in
advertising –
page 42
Using emotive
language –
page 44

Topics
- Encouraging more students at your school to buy school lunches
- Encouraging more students to travel to school on foot or by bicycle
  (but not by car)

Audience
Students of your age

Style
- Informal and informative
- Factual and persuasive

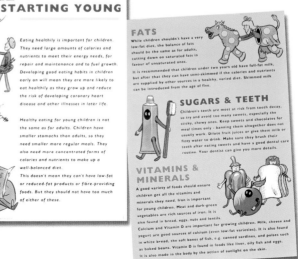

Writing a brochure

Introduction

How does a brochure differ from a leaflet?

Leaflets are small-scale texts (often one or two sides of A4). **Brochures** are booklets. Both use design features (images, different font styles and so on) to communicate their message. They are usually designed to inform or persuade.

Brochures are used to advertise new cars, schools, supermarkets, charities, holidays, and many other products.

Getting started

Brochures are often designed to appear chiefly **informative**: they contain tables of information and statistics about products or places they are advertising. But they are also intended to **persuade** us to buy their product, which is why their language often uses words associated with advertising.

1   Vocabulary

Holiday brochures use clichés (well-worn words and phrases) to conjure up powerfully attractive images of distant locations:

2   Sentence structure

Notice the sentence patterns that frequently occur in holiday brochures.

Imperatives (telling the reader what to do):

Declarative sentences (in particular, descriptions of places):

Majestic, snow-clad peaks dominate the horizon.

Time has passed by this place of peaceful charms.

Its quality hotels are renowned for their friendly service and high standards.

3   Style

This will depend on the audience, topic and purpose. Here is an extract from a holiday brochure aimed at young readers:

2wentys Flights are ready to **blast off** again for Summer 99.

It's a new concept in **flying** where we give you what you want

(not what some old gipper wants). Let's face it, if you're flying to Ibiza

it's **Sasha** and **Digweed** not **Mozart** and **Bach** you're after.

A brochure aimed at a different age-group, or people with different interests, would use a much more formal style.

Writing practice

30

Read the information panel below about the made-up holiday resort of Stalinos. Using the information here, write a 100-word passage of continuous prose (rather than bullet-points) for a holiday brochure on Stalinos aimed at young readers.
Use the language points in this unit to help you get the style right.

To bring your brochure extract to life, you'll need to get the sentence style right and choose lively, vivid vocabulary.

SEE ALSO:
Thinking about audience and register – page 10
Using word-play in headlines and slogans – page 34
Persuasive language in advertising – page 42
Using emotive language – page 44

Stalinos
* Hot climate, lively night-life, good facilities
* *** and **** hotels, all with pools
* modern self-catering facilities
* beaches, sailing, wind-surfing, scuba-diving
* local and international food

Writing a speech

Introduction

Speeches are still used as a way of informing and persuading people. They occur in politics, in education, at weddings and business events.

A good speech sounds like a speech, not an essay. It uses the rhythms of language to create its effects.

Getting started

Look at these extracts from a speech by Sue Suter, a polio sufferer who talks about conquering disabilities. See if you can find techniques you might use in your own speech-writing.

1 Opening

Ladies and gentleman, this is not a 'woe is me' speech. It is, however, about boat rocking. And it is about universal truths that women with disabilities have learned through a common experience. One of America's greatest boat rockers is Judy Heumann. She couldn't join you today. But she felt strongly about this conference. And she wanted to send a representative in her place. I hope to do her – and you – justice.

Notice:

- the way she addresses her audience ('Ladies and gentlemen', giving a formal, polite beginning)
- the short opening sentence to catch the listeners' attention
- the longer sentences to create different rhythms (look at the third sentence)
- the use of the conjunctions 'And' and 'But' to join ideas together and help the listener follow the thread of the speech
- the use of parenthesis ('– and you –') for emphasis.

2 Developing a personal tone

I contracted polio when I was two years old. I don't remember it. But I do remember my parents telling me about the advice that the doctor gave when it was time to take me home from the hospital. He told them, 'Just put her in bed. She's going to be staying there the rest of her life.'

Notice:
- the reference to herself, getting listeners on her side
- the short sentences for clarity
- the longer third sentence to add variety.

3 Making a powerful conclusion

Groups and individuals make a difference. And I believe with all my heart that it can happen again. We women with disabilities have the same hopes and dreams and ambitions as our non-disabled sisters. We are neither weak or heroic. We are normal. And we are boat rockers.

Notice:
- the emphasis on emotion: 'I believe with all my heart'
- the way she makes her audience identify with her message: 'we women'
- the way she draws people together: 'our non-disabled sisters'
- the use of short sentences for emphasis
- the way her text echoes the introduction: 'we are boat rockers'
- the repetition of the pronoun 'we'.

Writing practice

31 32

33 34

Choose one of the topics below and write a speech using the techniques discussed above. Write it in four sections, with the aim of persuading your audience to agree with your opinion.
- Plan an introduction, which tells your audience about your topic.
- Introduce your personal experience and opinions.
- Provide facts and statistics to support your opinion. A number of factsheets are provided in the accompanying Writing Frames book.
- Give a conclusion, showing why your audience should agree with you.

SEE ALSO: Thinking about audience and register – page 10 Using emotive language – page 44

Topics
1 Why schools will become less important as people have more technology at home for self-guided learning.
2 Why young people in the UK should be given more responsibility at an earlier age.
3 Why school uniform is / is not a good idea.

Writing autobiography

Introduction

An autobiography is writing about your own life. You might be asked to write about your early memories, or about an event that changed your life; or you might be asked to write the first chapter of your autobiography.

One key challenge with autobiographical writing is how to make it interesting to your reader – someone who may know nothing about you until they begin reading.

Your own life story may be fascinating to you and, perhaps, to your family, but how can you make it equally appealing to people who hardly know you?

It can be a problem even to get started. The obvious starting-point would be with your birth:

> I was born in Stafford, in the Midlands, in October 1962. I was born at 5.30 in the morning. My parents were going to call me John, but my older brother suggested Geoffrey.

How well does this work as a starting-point? Does it make you want to read on?

Answer: probably not.

Getting started

If you do end up writing about your birth, one way of making it more interesting is by adding emotional details rather than just facts. Here's an example:

> I was an unexpected third child. My mother was 43 and felt unwell. She went to the doctor thinking she had a heavy cold, only to learn that she was five months pregnant. That was a jolt to her system. My brother quickly began planning names. He wanted me named after famous footballers…

Notice how this immediately becomes more individual, less bland.

Detail is one key to writing a successful autobiography. The other is interesting phrasing: try to write an opening sentence that makes the reader want to read on… like this:

> *My father's father was said to come from East Anglia, which at one time I took to be some remote and savage mountain or desert region...*
>
> — Kingsley Amis

> My first ambition was to be an orphan. During the war of '39-45, Liverpool was a good place to be. All routine was broken by the fear of death from the Germans' bombs.
>
> —Tom Baker

> We are going by car from Bulaq Dakhur to Heliopolis. I am in the back. The leather of the seats sticks to my bare legs.
>
> —Penelope Lively

Writing practice

35 36 Write the opening of your own autobiography. Before you begin, decide whether you want to start with
- the day you were born
- a detail of your early memories (as Kingsley Amis and Tom Baker do)
- an incident from your childhood (as Penelope Lively does).

Then do some research. Find out from someone about the day you were born – what the weather was like, what the hospital was like, what you looked like, and so on. Ask people at home about incidents from your early childhood.

Then work on creating a startling, interesting opening sentence.

Use details to get the reader involved in your account.

Show your first paragraph to a friend and get some feedback on whether s/he would want to read on.

Aim to write three or four paragraphs in total, using really vivid vocabulary.

Writing a diary

Introduction

Diaries can be used for private writing, keeping a record of our thoughts and feelings. They are used in English assignments to let you write about yourself, or to imagine you are a character in a text. Real and fictional diaries can create powerful effects.

Getting started

Compare these versions of a moment in the life of Kate. The first version is written in the third person:

Kate's father received a letter that would change her life about three months later. He was going to take a new job that would take the family to Glasgow. She did not realize how quickly the time would go. When she first heard the news she was very upset. She did not like the idea of moving to a strange place, with strange new faces and – worst of all – a new school.

Notice:
- we look in on Kate's thoughts and feelings from the outside
- the writing feels formal, although it describes an upsetting event
- the events are told in the past tense (e.g. 'didn't' rather than 'doesn't'), making them seem distant from the present
- the writer uses third person pronouns – 'she', 'he' – so that we don't feel fully involved.

This style is excellent for some types of writing but here, it reduces the impact of the emotions Kate feels.

Now compare her diary version:

3 April

Dad received a letter today. I already know it's going to change my life. We always knew a new job would mean changes, but it's going to be a bigger change than I thought – a move to Glasgow. Until today it didn't seem real. I can't really take it in. I hate the idea of moving to a strange place... new friends, etc. But now I know it's going to happen.

Notice:
- we quickly understand the writer's feelings
- we can see her thoughts clearly because she uses her own words

• she is able to use more informal sentence styles and vocabulary.

Kate's diary is fairly **informal**. It is, of course, possible for diaries to be much more **formal** (a), or much more **informal** (b), by varying the vocabulary and sentence structure:

a

3 April

My father received a letter today, one that will undoubtedly change my life in approximately three months.

b

3 April

My dad got a letter today that's going to change my life in three months or so.

Writing practice

Using the notes below, write two diary entries, each by a fictitious (made-up) character – in other words, not yourself.

For the first one, imagine the character uses a really informal style. Think of a name for the character and try writing the entry.

Then imagine someone who uses a much more formal style. Experiment with different ways of writing the diary entry.

Use the two opening sentences below to get you started.

30 July

• last night of holidays
• starting new school tomorrow
• looking forward to it but also nervous
• have got uniform laid out on bed and all books, etc., ready
• wondering what the first day will be like
• afraid you won't be able to sleep

SEE ALSO: Formal language (and when to use it) – page 12 Informal language and when to use it – page 14

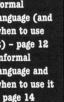

DIARY I (INFORMAL STYLE)

Can't believe the holidays are finished already...

Diary 2 (FORMAL STYLE)

The end of the holidays has come, and tomorrow a new phase of my life begins...

Writing a formal letter

Introduction

Formal letters are written to people we do not know well. There are two main things you need to get right:

- the style – formal but not stuffy
- the layout – clear and businesslike.

Many students are better at getting the layout right than the style, even though it's the written style of a text that often has the biggest impact.

Getting started

1 Style

If you have to write a **formal** letter, this will have an effect on your choice of **vocabulary** and your **sentence structure**.

Vocabulary will usually be more formal than you would use in everyday conversation – like this:

Everyday conversation	More formal register
Thanks	Thank you
Good luck	Best wishes
Loads of	Many
Great fun	Very enjoyable

Sentence structures will often be more complex, less conversational:

More conversational register	More formal register
Great seeing you on Wed. Not long enough though – hope we'll get more time next time!	It was very good to see you on Wednesday. However I hope we will get more time together next time.

Look at what happens in a formal letter when you get the register wrong:

Dear Ms Barns

I'm not at all happy about this jam I bought and nor's my mum. She's fuming about it in fact because when she opened the lid there was something nasty inside it and we couldn't work out what it was for ages, so that's pretty terrible for a start, isn't it?

Notice:
- how the style feels more like conversation than writing
- how ideas are joined by conjunctions 'and' and 'but', making the letter feel less structured
- how the use of elision makes it more informal ('it's' and 'nor's')
- how the vocabulary is very informal (e.g. 'fuming').

A more formal register might work like this:

> Dear Ms Barns,
>
> I am writing to complain about a jar of jam my mother bought this week.
> When she opened the jar, she was horrified to find that it contained an object which we were unable to identify.

2   Layout

Layout of formal letters is easy:
- your address goes at the top left, followed by the date
- on the right: the name, job title and address of the person you are writing to
- start with 'Dear Mr/Mrs/Ms [last name]'
- end with 'Yours sincerely' if you know the recipient's name, or 'Yours faithfully' if you don't
- sign at the bottom.

Writing practice

37

Take the letter above and continue it in a formal style.

Addressee:
Ms D Barns, Customer Relations Manager, Fresh Fruit Conserves, Clover Road, Cheadle, CH17 2GB

Complaint:
- Strange object in jam. Seemed furry with small legs.
- Returned to local supermarket – they said to contact the manufacturer.
- You phoned the customer careline and the person who answered treated it as a joke.
- You think you should at least receive refund of money, plus a replacement jar.

SEE ALSO: Formal language (and when to use it) – page 12

Writing an informal letter

Introduction

Informal letters are written to people we know. That still means there can be quite a range of informal styles. A thank-you letter to a distant aunt will use a different register from a note passed to a best friend.

In general, the layout of informal letters is less important. For example, in a very informal letter you will not bother about including your own address or the address of the person you are writing to. You will probably just write the date and then begin your message.

Getting started

An informal letter to someone in your family might look like this:

> Your address
> Date
>
> Dear Auntie Helen,
>
> Thank you very much for the....
>
> Lots of love / Best wishes / See you soon
>
> First name

Notice:
- there is still a clear layout to the letter
- it uses more informal vocabulary than you would expect in a business letter (for example, 'Lots of love')
- it finishes on an informal note, with just your first name.

You might sometimes be asked to write informal letters, either to real people, or as part of a unit of work in English (for example, 'Write to the character of Lyra in *Northern Lights* saying what you think she should do next').

The **language features** of an informal letter will include:
- more informal greetings ('Dear [first name]')
- a more conversational sentence structure (for example, clauses joined together by 'and' and 'but')

- more informal vocabulary (for example, 'fantastic' rather than 'really impressive')
- use of elisions ('won't' rather than 'will not'; 'it's' rather than 'it is')
- a more informal sign-off ('See you soon', 'All the best').

Writing practice

38

Look at this spoof thank-you letter which has been written in a very formal style. It sounds impersonal and pompous. How would you write it in an informal style suitable to an uncle whom you see just once or twice a year? Feel free to edit it and rewrite it in any way you wish.

> 72 Beyton Green
> Beyton
> Suffolk
> IP31 8TY
> July 31 1999
>
> James Ratcliffe Esq
> 13 Sunny Vale Road
> Edinburgh
> EH10 6PB
>
> Dear Uncle James
> It was with enormous pleasure that I received your unexpected gift. It was delivered by the postman at 8.25 yesterday morning.
>
> The choice of CDs is truly inspired. As I am sure you are aware, there has recently been a revival of interest in ABBA; therefore to possess my very own copy of Abba Gold is indeed a treat. Thank you also for the Black Sabbath CD and T-shirt which, as you say, summons up some of the glorious days of your own youth.
>
> I certainly enjoyed a pleasant birthday. My friends and I went out for pizza at a nearby establishment where I found their American Hot pizza to be exquisitely cooked. Then we went to see a film.
>
> My sincere thanks once again for your kindness.
>
> Yours truly,
>
> Nicholas

Informal language (and when to use it) – page 14

Writing a summary

Introduction

People are asked to write summaries for all kinds of reasons. A sub-editor on a newspaper or magazine may have the job of reducing the overall length of a story so that it fits the space available. Someone in business may be asked to provide a summary of a lengthy report to make discussion quicker for others who may not have read the full report. A film critic may want to summarize the storyline of a film so that readers know what it is about.

There is no single way of summarizing a text:

- The sub-editor will probably start at the end of the story, deleting paragraphs from the bottom which carry detail and quotation, leaving the main outline of the story at the top.
- The business executive may read the whole report and reduce it to a page of bullet-points by making judgements about what is important and what isn't.
- The critic will aim to reduce a two-hour storyline to three sentences or so by cutting out all background information and concentrating purely on the main events in the plot.

Getting started

Some hints for summarizing:

1. Be clear about your purpose and audience. If your purpose is to provide key points, you'll produce a very short summary. If your audience already knows about the topic, you can afford to be very brief. If not, you'll need to give more detail.
2. Know your format. If you have to write in sentences and paragraphs, your summary will probably use more words than bullet-points of key facts.
3. If you have been asked to summarize a text:
   a) Decide which parts of the text are essential information (new stage in a story; new information about a character; key facts in a report). Highlight them as you read, so that you begin the process of marking out the main parts of the text.
   b) Aim to change the words of the original: cut out unnecessary words, simplify vocabulary and shorten sentences. For example, the sentence 'It was, on the whole, fear of diving that finally led Ted Sanders to change career' might become: 'Fear of diving finally led Ted Sanders to change career'.

4   Know your target length – a page, 200 words – and be ruthless in sticking to it.

Writing practice

39   Look at this text from a biography of the actor Clint Eastwood, about the first part of his acting career. Use the text to practise your summarizing skills. (A copy which you can mark on is provided in the Writing Frames book.)

The first time he spoke lines to a camera, he blew them. A couple of pictures later he spoke his lines perfectly, but he was buried so deep in a dark scene that he couldn't be seen. Toward the end of his first year as an actor, he had a nice little scene with a major star on a major production, and he found a good-looking pair of glasses that he thought gave him a bit of character. But Rock Hudson thought the same thing when he saw the kid wearing them, and Clint had to surrender his specs to the leading man.

This was Clint Eastwood's life as an eager young contract player at Universal circa 1955, and it turned out to be a short one – the studio dropped him after a year and a half. On his own, he did what young actors do: played scenes in acting classes, worked out at the gym, went on auditions, did odd jobs (mostly he dug swimming pools under the hot sun of the San Fernando Valley). Every once in a while he got an acting job – on *Highway Patrol*, on *Death Valley Days*. Once a big time show flew him east to work on location on *West Point Stories*. He got to bully James Garner on an episode of *Maverick*. A couple of times his heart leapt up: he got good billing in a feature, *The First Travelling Saleslady*, playing opposite Carol Channing; and he thought for a while that he had one of the leads in another feature, *Lafayette Escadrille*. But the first film was a flop, and he had to settle for a much smaller role in the second. When he finally got a decent part in a movie, it was in a B western so bad it almost caused him to quit the business.

Writing a review – page 24

1   Summarize the information in five bullet-points.
2   You are writing the notes for a video booklet to accompany a new collection of classic Clint Eastwood movies. You need 100 words about the start of his career to go with the first film he starred in, *A Fistful of Dollars*.
3   Write a 50-word answer to the question, 'How did Clint Eastwood get into the movie industry?'

Writing instructions

Introduction

Instructions appear in all kinds of texts: in cookery books, on leaflets telling you how to make or do something, on the side of medicines, with games and kits, in booklets showing people how to programme their videos…

Many of us are impatient with instructions. We want to get on and do things rather than read about how to do them. Therefore the best instructional writing is clear, direct, and laid out very logically.

Getting started

Instructions are especially important to people who are making or putting something together. Look at the instructions on the opposite page for fitting a light on an outside wall.

1 Language

How clear is the language of these instructions?

Notice that:
- the vocabulary is quite technical – 'adjacent', 'conduit box', 'gasket'
- the tone is quite impersonal – no mention of 'you'
- most sentences begin with a verb, or adverb then verb ('ensure… carefully identify') to create a feeling of directness
- the imperative form of the verb is often used (the verb at the start of the sentence, telling readers what to do: 'Lift the… Hold the… Add…').

2 Layout

Is the overall layout of the text helpful?

Notice that:
- the text is quite cramped
- all the writing is in capital letters (rather than capital letters at the start of sentences and for names, as we might normally expect).

EXTERNAL WALL LAMP

INSTALLATION INSTRUCTIONS

THIS WALL LIGHT IS DESIGNED FOR OUTDOOR USE AND IS SUITABLE FOR MOUNTING ON EXPOSED WALLS. HOWEVER IT IS NOT RECOMMENDED FOR CORROSIVE ENVIRONMENTS.

IT IS VITALLY IMPORTANT THAT THESE INSTRUCTIONS ARE READ IN THEIR ENTIRETY AND ANY ILLUSTRATIONS STUDIED BEFORE COMMENCING THE INSTALLATION.

IF IN ANY DOUBT OVER THE INSTALLATION CONSULT A QUALIFIED ELECTRICIAN.

1. **ENSURE THAT THE ELECTRICAL SUPPLY IS TURNED OFF**.

2. ENSURE THE EXISTING CIRCUIT TO WHICH THE FITTING IS TO BE CONNECTED HAS BEEN INSTALLED AND FUSED IN ACCORDANCE WITH CURRENT L.E.E. WIRING REGULATIONS.

3. POSITION THE LIGHT WHERE DESIRED AND CONFIRM THE METHOD OF FIXING WHICH WILL BE REQUIRED: WOODSCREW FOR WOOD, WOODSCREW/WALL PLUG FOR BRICK OR MASONRY, SPECIAL CAVITY FIXINGS FOR CAVITY WALLS OR MACHINE SCREWS FOR EXTERNAL WALL BOX. IMPORTANT: NO FIXING SCREWS ARE SUPPLIED.

4. CAREFULLY IDENTIFY THE LOCATION OF THE MAINS SUPPLY CABLE AND ANY OTHER CABLES IN THE AREA WHICH YOU INTEND TO FIX THE LIGHT IN ORDER TO AVOID DAMAGE DURING INSTALLATION.

5. ENSURE THAT THE MAINS ELECTRICITY SUPPLY IS ADJACENT TO THIS FIXING POINT.

6. IF REMOVING AN EXISTING FITTING, CAREFULLY NOTE ALL WIRING CONNECTIONS. RECORD WHICH OF THE HOUSE WIRES ARE CONNECTED TO WHICH TERMINAL ON THE LIGHT.

7. IF *EXTERNAL* MOUNTING IS SELECTED IT IS VITAL THAT THE WALL PLATE IS ONLY FIXED TO AN APPROVED BESA/CONDUIT BOX AND THAT A RUBBER GASKET IS FITTED TO PROVIDE A WATERTIGHT SEAL. ALTERNATIVELY CONNECTION MAY BE MADE *INTERNALLY* BY FEEDING THE EXTRA LONG CABLE THROUGH YOUR WALL (SEE BELOW).

3 Audience

Based on looking at the language and layout of the text, who do you think it is aimed at?
- Qualified electricians?
- Knowledgeable non-specialists?
- People with little electrical experience?

How can you tell?
Think of three ways you might make the instructions easier to follow.

Now compare these cookery instructions from the *Blue Peter* website.

Bonfire Brownies

Ingredients
100 grams butter
225 grams golden caster sugar
40 grams cocoa powder
2 eggs
1tsp vanilla essence
50 grams self raising flour
50 grams chocolate chips

Method
Beat the eggs and add the sugar, mix until smooth.

Melt your butter in a pan, take it off the heat and add 40 grams of cocoa powder. (You need a strong flavour so it needs to be cocoa powder and not drinking chocolate.) Mix together getting rid of any lumps.

Add this mixture to your egg mixture and stir thoroughly and then add your drops of vanilla essence.

Mix in 50 grams of self raising flour (this needs to be sieved gradually so that your mixture doesn't go lumpy).

Simon and Matt's special secret ingredient is 50 grams of chocolate chips – this makes it really chocolatey, the way we like it here at Blue Peter! Mix them all in.

Your mixture will be really sticky now so grease your baking tin.

Cook in a medium to hot oven at gas mark 4, 180 Celsius for about 25 mins. If you have a fan oven be careful because they will cook much quicker. Simon and Matt had a disaster the first time they tried to cook them because the oven was too hot! However tempting they may seem, they should not be eaten until they are cooled!

Good luck with the brownies… let us know if you enjoyed cooking them!

Notice:
- the straightforward vocabulary and short paragraphs for clarity
- the personal tone – for example, references to 'Simon and Matt'
- the use of exclamation marks to give a jokey, informal feel
- hints given in brackets to show that they are less important pieces of information.

The jokey tone, the use of exclamation marks, and the mention of the 'disaster' show that the subject matter is not serious. We wouldn't expect to find features like these on, for instance, the side of a medicine bottle.

Writing practice

40

Write instructions for one of the following:
1. Making perfect tea
2. Cleaning your teeth thoroughly

Imagine your readers don't know much about either process. They are relying on you for very clear guidance.

Decide whether to make the style of your instructions formal or informal.

SEE ALSO: Formal language (and when to use it) – page 12 Informal language (and when to use it) – page 14

Thinking up ideas for stories

Introduction

A blank piece of paper – or a computer screen – can be a threatening thing. In class, in an exam, or for homework you might have to write a story, and all you have is whiteness in front of you. How can you get started?

Here are some techniques that professional writers use to think up ideas:

I always begin with a character, or characters, and then try to think up as much action for them as possible.

— John Irving

With me, a story usually begins with a single idea or memory or mental picture. The writing of the story is simply a matter of working up to that moment, to explain why it happened or what caused it to follow.

— William Faulkner

All my books literally come to me in the form of a sentence, an original sentence which contains the entire book.

— Raymond Federman

I KNOW VERY DIMLY WHEN I START WHAT'S GOING TO HAPPEN. I JUST HAVE A VERY GENERAL IDEA AND THEN THE THING DEVELOPS AS I WRITE.

— Aldous Huxley

Mostly it's just a first line or an image or a vague sense of a situation.

— Bobbie Ann Mason

If I didn't know the ending of a story, I wouldn't begin. I always write my last line, my last paragraphs, my last page first.

— Katherine Anne Porter

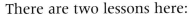

There are two lessons here:

1. There is no single way of getting started on a story.
2. Even long-established writers find this part of the process difficult.

Getting started

Based on the comments of these writers, here are some ways to think up ideas for stories. See which technique best suits your own way of working.

Character	Examples
Think of a central character.	**A:** Boy – 15 – popular and successful – moves to new school – feels like he's an outsider – gets drawn into the wrong crowd – relationship with parents begins to fall apart…
What is the frustration or conflict in her/his life?	
What is s/he like? What does s/he look like?	**B:** Elderly woman who feels abandoned by her children. Decides to teach them a lesson…
What's her/his background?	
Which other character will s/he come into contact with?	
Create a mini-biography using bullet-points or in note form.	

Setting	Examples
Think of an opening location. Be bold and creative – don't just think of a setting you're very familiar with. Use your imagination to create somewhere.	**A:** Desert where small plane suddenly touches down…
	B: Forest which someone suddenly runs into and scrambles up a tree for cover…
Visualize it. Think of the details. Bring the scene to life in your mind.	**C:** Quiet shop where armed police suddenly walk in with an urgent message…
Draw a map or sketch of it.	
Then think what will happen here – an event – something that surprises the reader.	

Plot

Think of a basic step-by-step storyline. At the heart of it there should be some conflict.

Plan the first stage. Think about what happens as a result. Then what?

Try to choose next steps that might surprise the reader.

Show your stages as a flow-chart or diagram – no need for any detail yet.

You might start with the final step in the story – how it will end.

Examples

Man wires up his house with high-tech security devices.

Burglar breaks in whilst the man's still testing them.

Burglar is trapped in the house – man doesn't know. Man sets alarms and goes away.

Burglar tries to find a way of breaking *out* of the house without setting off the alarms.

Opening sentences

Experiment with different opening sentences. Use them to kick-start your story or establish setting.

Try a short sentence with almost no description.

Try a sentence which contains pronouns ('he', 'she', 'they', 'we') rather than revealing the names of characters – this will create suspense.

Experiment by adding details to the sentence, changing the viewpoint, so that you try out the same scene from the point of view of different characters.

Examples

A: The turbulence outside the aircraft was getting worse.

B: The turbulence outside the Boeing 747 was getting worse, jolting Mrs Wilson's Diet Coke out of her hand.

C: As he pushed the cabin door closed behind him, he felt the force of the turbulence and knew he'd made a terrible mistake.

D: A small hatch underneath a Boeing 747 is vital to its safety. Today, Len Seymour's mind was on other things – his marriage, his kids – and the hatch remained unchecked. In the control tower Sarah Burrows was giving Captain Fuller permission to taxi.

Writing practice

41 Use each of the techniques given in the writing grids (character, setting, plot, opening sentences) to try out ideas for a story. Your aim is not to write a story at this point, but to find ways of generating story ideas which work best for you.

Hints:

- Be critical of anything you write. Keep nagging away at it, rewriting it, changing words, cutting unnecessary words.
- The best writing usually has specific details of people and places – don't be too general.
- Share your page of story ideas with other people in your group and talk about which techniques you found most helpful.

Planning a storyline

Introduction

Writer James N Frey has written a book called *How to Write a Damn Good Novel*. Based on his ideas, we could say that a good storyline will have three basic ingredients:

1 A story is a sequence of events, with each step depending on the previous one, like the story of Little Red Riding Hood.

2 A story must contain events that are worth reading about.

3 A story contains interesting characters who are changed by the end. Little Red Riding Hood learns not to trust strangers.

Getting started

Now look at how planning a storyline can help you to tell your story more creatively. Take the Little Red Riding Hood example. It is a story in five steps. You could start at step one:

> Once upon a time, a little girl called Little Red Riding Hood decided to go and visit her grandmother...

Or you could start at step two, giving the step one information as background information or as a flashback:

> Little Red Riding Hood was walking deeper into the forest when she heard a sound behind a tree. A wolf stepped out. Suddenly she wished that she hadn't chosen to visit her grandmother today. It had seemed such a good idea at the time...

Or you could start at any other stage in the story – even the last one – and tell it from someone else's point of view:

> Ralph Tate was alone today because his partner was unwell. He'd just finished his morning's work - cutting up a pile of tree trunks for the manor house - when he heard a sound of screaming. He looked towards the old cottage and noticed the door was open...

Or you could tell the story in two or even three narratives, cutting between the two:

> Ralph Tate arrived at work and was immediately disappointed. His partner, Seb, was off sick today. He'd have to work alone. 'That's all I need,' he thought to himself, as he looked at the huge pile of logs that needed cutting up for this evening's event at the manor.
>
> As she pushed back the window of her bedroom, Little Red Riding Hood had to close her eyes against the bright sunlight. 'A perfect day for a walk to Grandma's,' she thought, and quickly got dressed.
>
> Deep in the forest a wolf was sitting alone. He too was thinking what a promising day it seemed.

Notice:
- these different ways of telling the story create different effects
- you can tell the same story from different points of view
- the use of details – e.g. the name of the woodcutter and his partner – brings a story to life
- you need to work out the basic story steps before you can plan how to tell the story.

Writing practice

42

Take another fairy tale – for example, Goldilocks and the Three Bears or Jack and the Beanstalk. Then:
- break the story into three to five steps
- experiment with telling the opening of the story in three different ways:
  1 from the beginning
  2 from the second or third story step
  3 using two or three narratives to show different characters' points of view.

SEE ALSO:
Building a storyline – page 92
Making a chronological story interesting – page 94
Writing non-chronological stories – page 96
Exploring viewpoint – page 98

Knowing your audience

Introduction

Audience is always a really important factor for a writer. Who you are writing for will affect the way you approach your story.

These are some of the most likely audiences you will be asked to write for in school:

'School' audiences
Your teacher
An examiner

'Real' audiences
Young children
Older readers
Students of a similar age

Getting started

1   Teacher/examiner audiences

This is the main audience most students have in school for their writing. Your teacher will set up a topic, give you guidance, and then give you feedback. Writing for her or him will usually be fairly straightforward because you will know what s/he expects.

Writing for an examiner (for example in the Year 9 Tests) is more demanding because
a)   you're writing under test conditions
b)   the topic will have been set up in much less detail
c)   you will not know the person you're writing for.

Some hints:
- Examiners mark hundreds of scripts at a time. They look for writing which is lively, entertaining and accurate. Do not be afraid to take risks in your writing – for example, trying out different story structures or playing with point of view.
- Try to write visually: give details about appearances, textures, and colours to draw the examiner into your writing.
- Aim to write a really interesting first sentence: it will build your confidence and make the examiner notice your work.
- Pay careful attention to your vocabulary. Make yourself pause and think of exactly the word you need, not the first one that enters your head. This will make your writing sharper and more vivid.
- Spend time checking through the accuracy of your work: this is going to be especially important for examination assignments where marks are awarded for accuracy.

2 'Real' audiences

Compare these two story openings written for a child aged 5–7:

> **Good example:**
> Danny was worrying about something.
> Danny was often worrying about something. Today he was worrying about the shadow at the foot of his bed.

Notice:
- the writer introduces the character straight away
- the use of repetition will help a young reader to follow the story
- short sentences give clarity
- the vocabulary will be familiar to a child
- the interesting storyline will make a child want to read on.

> **Poor example:**
> The shadow at the foot of Danny's bed continued to trouble him as he lay there wondering what it might be.

Notice:
- the sentence is too long
- the vocabulary (e.g. 'wondering') feels hard in a long sentence
- the way the text is written feels too adult for the target age-group.

Writing practice

43

Take the opening of this story and rewrite it for a teenage audience. The current version is too babyish – in language and emotional level. Experiment with changes to content, characters, setting, vocabulary, and sentences so that it suits the target audience better.

SEE ALSO:
Knowing your audience – page 74
Building a storyline – page 92

Sarah sat on the beach. She watched the waves. They were really big. It was early morning and the whole village seemed to be waking up around her. She loved being on holiday in France. The sky was bright blue and it promised to be a glorious day.

At the back of the beach a dark car suddenly drove up. Three men got out. They ran into a small shop. Sarah could hear shouting. She was very worried. She wondered what to do.

Presenting characters by telling

Introduction

One of the chief reasons we read stories – or watch them on television or in the cinema – is to see the way characters behave. We get to know them at the start of the story; we follow their progress; we get involved with them. You can see how involved some soap opera viewers become – when a character dies, they send flowers and cards, as if the fictional character is a real person.

There are all kinds of ways of presenting characters in stories. The most direct way is by **telling** your reader about them.

Getting started

'Telling' is the oldest style of presenting characters. For as long as people have told stories, they have told their audience what the characters are like. For example, it's the style we use in jokes.

> **There was this man who was really mean and really ugly...**

The advantage of this style is that it's quick and straightforward. It leaves little room for the listener or reader to misunderstand you.

'Telling' allows you to tell an audience:
- what a character looks like
- how s/he speaks
- how s/he behaves
- her/his background
- what s/he is thinking
- what her/his hopes, fears, desires are
- what motivates her/him.

'Telling' usually uses statements about what a person thinks and feels:

> Her face was old now, a used crumpled envelope, but a child still looked out from her eyes.
>
> Nina Bawden, *George Beneath a Paper Moon*

Notice:
- how the writer helps us to visualize what the character looks like
- how simple and yet powerful the vocabulary is

- how the comparison – 'a used crumpled envelope' – helps us to see what the character looks like.

Oscar Wilde's classic children's story, *The Selfish Giant*, also uses techniques of telling. Look at these two extracts from different points in the story, and see how the writer **tells** us about the Giant's:

- appearance
- emotions
- behaviour
- personality.

Beginning:

He was a very selfish giant…

End:

The Giant was very kind to all the children, yet he longed for his first little friend…
Years went by, and the Giant grew very old and feeble. He could not play about any
more, so he sat in a huge armchair, and watched the children at their games, and
admired his garden.

Writing practice

44

Choose someone you know well – a friend, parent or close relative – and write about her/him as a character in a story. Imagine that the character is being introduced at the start of a chapter. Present her/him in a situation and tell the reader about her/his:

- appearance (clothes, height, build, body language, stance, gestures)
- mannerisms or habits
- thoughts (about her/himself, about what has just happened, about the future, about other people)
- hopes (in the near future, in the longer term)

and so on.

Write it as a paragraph. Then read it back. What if you were to read a paragraph like this at the start of a story? How well does it work? The advantage of telling is that it is a very direct way of giving your reader information, but what are the disadvantages?

SEE ALSO: Using description to reveal more about a character – page 80
Using dialogue to reveal character – page 84

Presenting characters by showing

Introduction

If 'telling' is the most direct way of giving the reader information about a character, 'showing' can make the reader feel more actively involved in a story.

Telling is when the writer gives us statements about what a character thinks or feels. **Showing** is when the writer describes the character's actions, leaving us to work out what s/he is thinking or feeling. For example:

Telling	Showing
As he cleared his desk, Peter was in a furious temper.	Peter cleared his desk, snatching at heaps of paper and hurling them into the bin.

Notice:
- with **telling** the reader knows exactly what Peter is feeling
- with **showing** we see how he behaves, but the writer leaves us to do more of the work. Clues like 'snatching' and 'hurling' suggest aggression and anger. From this we infer that Peter is in a furious temper.

Getting started

The secret of showing your reader what a character is like lies in choosing your vocabulary carefully. One word can be a vital clue to what a character is thinking or feeling.

Look at these examples and try to work out what clues the writer might be giving us about the character's thoughts, feelings, personality, or appearance. The first example is done for you.

45

Extract	Character point	Main clue
The man shuffled towards the run-down house.	The man is old or infirm.	'Shuffled' suggests he cannot walk well – because he is either old or ill.
Rita sat on the bottom step and placed her head in her hands.		
He sat outside the room and again touched his collar, then his tie.		
Kay moved quickly from the armchair to her desk. There she began writing frantically.		
As he listened to the student's story, Mr Parker's hands tightened.		

Writing practice

46

Notice how simply you can show a reader about a character:

> Andy yawned. 'You'll be lucky,' he said.

Character message: suggests boredom – lack of belief in the person he's talking to.

SEE ALSO: Using description to reveal more about a character – page 80
Using dialogue to reveal character – page 84

> Andy lowered his voice. 'You'll be lucky,' he whispered.

Character message: suggests secrecy, perhaps menace, or that they are being overheard.

Write five more sentences about Andy, changing the two highlighted elements in each sentence, and then saying what the character message might be. To get you started, try to show Andy as sarcastic and then really happy.

Using description to reveal more about a character

Introduction

Small details of description can be a really good way of telling your reader about your characters.

Take this example:

> **Serena sat in her car.**

What do we know about Serena?

We know what she is doing, but little else. Carefully-judged description can give the reader vital clues.

Getting started

Change the sentence to:

> **Serena sat in her Porsche.**

We begin to make judgements about Serena's background, her lifestyle and wealth.

What about:

> **Serena shifted uneasily in her Porsche. She looked in the rear mirror and lowered her head suddenly as if she were reading a book or magazine.**

We learn about:
- Serena's attitude (she seems nervy, worried)
- her lifestyle (her Porsche)
- her behaviour (but the writer keeps us guessing – what has she seen in the mirror? Why is she hiding her head?)

You can use all kinds of description to illuminate character:

Appearance
- Serena's sunglasses hid her concern.
- Her mouth turned down at the edges.

Setting
- The traffic roared past as she sat there [showing that she's isolated].
- The sky darkened [suggesting danger].

Actions

- She tapped her fingers rapidly on the dashboard [suggesting nervousness].
- She fumbled beneath the seat for her briefcase ['fumbled' suggests that she's in a rush].

Bystanders

Bystanders are other characters. You can use them to give information about your main character, or to show her from a different viewpoint:

- The man cleaning the window of the shop watched her light a cigarette.
- Jane Tate, walking to work, noticed a woman in sunglasses in a smart car and thought no more about it.

Hints

- Keep your details brief and precise – not great slabs of description.
- Keep description visual – appearances, textures, colours, movements – to help your reader see the scene
- Give specific details, e.g. 'a Porsche', 'a Vauxhall', rather than 'a car'. Details like these can tell us about a character. ('He ate his half-melted Kit-Kat' is more interesting than 'He ate his chocolate bar'.)

Writing practice

Practise using some of these techniques with the writing task below. Aim to produce a really lively, interesting piece of writing that would work well within a story.

Imagine a character waiting in a queue at a post office. He is in a terrible hurry to get money out, in order to go across the street to buy a phone. It is the last day of the sale and it is now 5.20. He has ten minutes to get the money, cross the street and buy the phone. Call him Steve Rawlins. Make up any other details.

Use descriptions of people and places, plus dialogue if you wish, to bring the scene alive.

Getting the amount of description right

Introduction

Different readers probably like different levels of description. In general, though, it seems that modern readers prefer the story to keep moving, rather than encounter big slabs of description.

One of the big dangers for new writers is that they tell the reader too much at once about people and places. With characters, this can really get in the way of the action, slowing the story down and leading to a loss of tension.

Here's how to get the balance right.

Getting started

When you know your character well, you can be tempted to try to tell your reader everything about her or him. This can really slow the pace of the story down, like this:

> Tom looked up and saw Mel, from his class, in the doorway. She was tall with fair hair. Today she was wearing grey jeans and a blue top. She was a friendly cheerful girl and her sense of humour meant she had lots of friends. She lived in a big house on Carter Street with her mum, who was a dentist, and her two brothers and her dog, Jip.
> 'Hi,' said Tom.

Notice:
- how much telling is going on here: the writer tells us what Mel looks like, where she lives, who she lives with, even what her mother's job is
- how this amount of description slows the whole story down by getting in the way.

You could cut all the description, like this:

> Tom looked up and saw Mel.
> 'Hi,' he said.

Notice that we lose all the visual detail of where the story takes place and who the characters are. We need more detail than this.

Alternatively, you could cut between description and action to create a more balanced effect, like this:

> Tom looked up and saw Mel, from his class, in the doorway.
> 'Hi,' he said.
> 'Hi. How are you?' she asked, and flicked her long fair hair our of her eyes.
> She was smiling. She was always smiling; Tom supposed that was one reason she was so popular.
> Tom shrugged his shoulders. 'Okay, I suppose.'
> Mel dug her hands into the pockets of her grey jeans. She looked at him. 'Something the matter?'
> 'It's okay,' said Tom, and he started to walk away.
> 'Tom, come on. There's obviously something wrong. Look, I can tell. You're behaving just like Alec when he's bothered about something.' Alec was Mel's brother, a year older than both her and Tom.

Notice:
- the cutting between description, dialogue and action
- how this creates pace and tension
- how the writer is still able to give details about Mel – but not all in one slab of description.

Writing practice

47

Here is another poor piece of descriptive writing. It makes a bad start to a story because it is so dull. See what you can do by rewriting it to create a more powerful opening to a story.

Remember to:
- get some action into the description – make people or animals **do** something
- make up some dialogue to change the rhythms of the writing
- avoid using the verb 'to be' ('was'/'is') too much
- choose words that create pictures in the reader's mind
- use similes if appropriate.

SEE ALSO: Using dialogue to reveal character – page 84

Jenkins was sitting in a seat in an aircraft. He was wearing a navy blue suit, though he wished that he had taken off his jacket. He had a tie on that had the logo of his company on it. It was an unusually hot day for Heathrow in the spring. The pilot was waiting for clearance to take off. The cabin crew had sealed the doors and were walking up and down to check that everyone had fastened their seatbelts. A man near the back was sweating and closing his eyes. A child at the front was yelling. Jenkins got out his newspaper and thought what a long flight it was going to be.

Using dialogue to reveal character

Introduction

Apart from showing and telling, writers also use dialogue to reveal what their characters are like. The words a character says can tell us a lot about their thoughts, feelings, and attitudes – and sometimes it tells us little. For example:

> 'Hi,' said Tom.
> 'Oh hi,' said Liz.
> 'How are you?' said Tom.
> 'Fine,' said Liz.
> 'Busy?' asked Tom.
> 'Quite,' replied Liz.

You can imagine that too much of this would be very dull.

Getting started

Look at how you could make the dialogue more interesting:

1 Building dialogue into the story

Dialogue in small or large slabs can feel too separate from the story. Cutting between dialogue, description and plot can add variety and pace. It can give the reader more detail about where a conversation is taking place, and show **how** the characters speak to each other, what their emotions are and what they are like as people.

> She hadn't noticed anyone come into the room.
> 'Hi,' said Tom.
> 'Oh hi,' said Liz, startled. She looked around the classroom to see if anyone was watching her.
> 'How are you?' said Tom, sitting on the edge of a desk.
> 'Fine,' said Liz.
> 'Busy?' asked Tom.
> 'Quite,' replied Liz, who was already packing away her books and papers.

Notice:

- how the scene comes to life more because we can visualize where it takes place
- how the dialogue is beginning to tell us more about the characters, indirectly – that she is nervous/reluctant to talk and he seems confident/arrogant.

2 Using 'said'

Writers sometimes worry about repeating the word 'said' when they write dialogue. In fact, readers often tune the word out as they read – they don't notice it. But sometimes you could choose another verb in order to reveal a character's mood or intentions. You could:

a) choose a verb which tells us more about the character's attitude – for example, 'muttered', 'whispered', 'agreed', 'shouted', 'remarked', 'replied', 'responded', 'uttered', 'declared', 'announced', 'disclosed', 'revealed', 'stated'.

b) sometimes just leave the 'said' part out altogether, making the reader work harder – like this:

> She hadn't noticed anyone come into the room.
> 'Hi,' said Tom.
> 'Oh hi,' muttered Liz, startled. She looked around the classroom to see if anyone was watching her.
> 'How are you?' Tom sat down on the edge of a desk.
> 'Fine.'
> 'Busy?' Tom was staring directly at her.
> 'Quite,' replied Liz, who was already packing away her books and papers.

Notice:

- how replacing 'said' with other verbs can add variety and tell us more about the character ('muttered' shows that Liz is not pleased to see Tom)
- how removing the 'said' altogether can increase the pace of the story and get the reader more involved.

48

Writing practice

Using the techniques listed in this section, breathe life into this piece of dialogue. You should be able to make it into an exciting section from a thriller. Imagine that the setting is a train carriage.

SEE ALSO: **Exploring viewpoint – page 98**

> 'Excuse me, is this your newspaper?' the man said.
> 'No,' I said.
> 'May I borrow it?' he said.
> 'Help yourself,' I said.
> 'You've seen this front page story about the attacks taking place on trains?'
> 'Yes,' I said.

Making places seem real

Introduction

Setting can be one of the most important ingredients in a story. The power of words allows writers to set their scenes anywhere – in this world, in the past, in the future, even in outer space. All the reader needs is imagination.

The range of settings you might use is enormous. For instance, you might choose a long bus queue on a wet night; an eerie burnt-out cottage in a wood; a busy football stadium; an empty theme park in winter; the inside of an alien space craft; or your own kitchen.

Getting started

How can you make these places seem real? You have an advantage with the last possibility – your own kitchen – because you know what it looks like. That's the first rule in creating settings: try to use places that you personally know, or adapt places to suit your story.

You will need also to concentrate on the style of your descriptions. Sentences which start 'There was… It was… There were…' are often a sign of dull descriptive writing.

Take this example – the opening of an imaginary story set at a funeral. It ought to be a gripping opening, but notice how passive description gets in the way:

> It was a bitterly cold day. Everyone was in black. The cars were black too. There were people standing around in a group waiting for the coffin. Crows were flying in the sky. It was really eerie.

This is a terrible opening. **Notice:**
- how many sentences start: 'it was… there were…'
- how the use of the verb 'to be' ('was' and 'were') reduces the power of the description – it isn't active enough
- how the writer **tells** us that it was eerie, rather than showing us.

Now look at the way a brilliant writer brings the scene to life. This is the opening to Susan Hill's novel, *Mrs de Winter*:

Repetition of emotive words adds to tension.

Vocabulary is simple but powerful.

Use of adverb 'suddenly' creates tension – something that breaks the atmosphere.

The movement of the crows and the way the writer imitates their sound makes them seem menacing.

The undertaker's men were like crows, stiff and black, and the cars were black, lined up beside the path that led to the church; and we, we too were black, as we stood in our pathetic, awkward group waiting for them to lift out the coffin and shoulder it, and for the clergyman to arrange himself, and he was another black crow in his long cloak. And then the real crows rose suddenly from the trees and from the fields, whirled up like scraps of blackened paper from a bonfire, and circled, caw-cawing above our heads.

Scene contains movement and action – the undertakers, the crowd of onlookers, the clergyman and the crows. We wonder who they all are and why they are here.

Similes help us to visualize the scene really powerfully.

Image of the 'blackened paper from a bonfire' is very effective – suggesting danger and creating a strong visual picture.

Writing practice

49 50

Use **one** of the tasks below to practise opening a story with a description of a character doing something in a setting. Aim to:
- make the character the central focus, carrying us into the story
- create the setting using visual language (make the reader see what you see)
- avoid slabs of description – use a light-touch approach
- give specific details – names of places, exact locations.

1 Two people are setting up a picnic in a place you know. The weather looks threatening.
2 You walk into your own home and find that the electricity and telephone are not working.

SEE ALSO: Getting the amount of description right – page 82
Writing strong story openings – page 102

Fitting characters into realistic settings

Introduction

Many stories need settings which are realistic – places that readers will feel are true-to-life and believable. One of the best ways of achieving this is by making sure your settings contain **specific details**.

Look at this example. Imagine I use my own office as the setting for a scene in a story. I'll call the central character Matthew. How well does this description work?

> Matthew sat at his desk with the computer in front of him. He had a drink and then made a telephone call. Then he decided he needed to get another section of the book completed, so he opened up a file and started typing.

This isn't terrible writing, but it isn't exciting. It doesn't get the reader involved or make us want to read on. So what is it lacking?

Getting started

Remember that to bring a setting to life, you do not need to write lengthy descriptions. The key way of making the setting feel real is by helping the reader to see it in her/his mind.

In particular, think about your reference to the different senses: sight, sound, smell, taste, texture. All of these could help you to create a convincing setting.

Instead of:	... you could say more about:
Matthew	What he looks like; how he's dressed; how he's feeling; why he's there; his habits; his posture, gestures and mannerisms; the bitter taste of his black coffee.
His desk	What else is on the desk; where the desk is in the room; the smell of the room – disinfectant, coffee; the shape, the texture, the age – polished, shiny, rough, scratched.
The computer	What type it is; what it looks like; what's on the screen; how old/new it is; how fast/powerful it is.
A telephone call	How he dials; who he dials; what he says; what his and the other person's voices sound like; how the phone ringer sounds; why he's calling.

... and so on.

You don't want to add detail about everything because the writing will become too stodgy, too difficult for the reader to follow. But helping the reader to imagine the scene by using references to the five senses should bring the writing to life:

> Matthew reluctantly sat down at his desk. He could barely see the surface for all the papers and Post-it notes that were scattered around. His battered PC sat humming, ready to start work. Matthew would do anything to avoid starting. He reached for the phone and hit one of the presets...

Notice:

- the details about the character: 'reluctantly', 'would do anything to avoid starting'
- the precise visual details to help the reader see the scene: scattered papers and Post-it notes, the 'battered PC'
- references to the senses – sounds, sight and texture
- the active verbs: 'reached', 'hit'.

Writing practice

51

Look at this extract. Again, it is unexciting and does not feel very real. Rewrite it to make it more realistic, using the techniques listed above.

> Jane was at the railway station. She was waiting for the next train to her home town. Lots of people were standing around on the platform and sitting in the waiting-room. A train sped through the station without stopping. Then there was an announcement saying that her train had been delayed because of a breakdown in Doncaster. It would be an hour late. Jane was very annoyed and went into the station buffet for a sandwich.

Some hints:

- Help the reader to visualize Jane: what does she look like?
- Give her some motivation: why is she travelling to Peterborough? Why is it important that she is there on time?
- Add some detail about the people on the station.
- Create an impression of the waiting-room – its heating, the colour of the walls, the people in there.
- Make the train passing through more dramatic.
- Bring the station announcement to life more by using direct speech.
- Show the reaction of the people – how they look and what they say.
- Create a picture of the station buffet as Jane goes in.

SEE ALSO:
Writing strong story openings
– page 102

89

Creating fantasy settings

Introduction

It is easy to assume that fantasy and science fiction stories use completely different techniques from stories with realistic settings. In fact, many of the same rules apply because readers need to believe in the worlds that are being described.

It is not easy to lay down rules about fantasy writing. There are so many different possible styles and approaches.

Getting started

Look at this opening to a story by Jan Mark:

> Arty said: 'I want to play in the street.'
> Arty's mother said, 'For heaven's sake stop whining and get out from under my feet.'

There is no way we would guess that this is an extract from a science fiction story. Look at the next paragraph and see what clues there are about the genre (or category) of the story:

> Arty squeezed past her, between the home laundry unit where the week's washing was twirling in its drum, and the fast food module, into the leisure area. There was not very much more space in there, for his elder brother Lance was lying on the floor playing chess with PREM, his Programmed Response Module.

Notice:
- the attention to familiar details – streets, chess, washing
- the mixture of action and description – Arty squeezing past his mother, moving from area to area. This helps us to see the scene and holds our interest in what is happening.

How can we begin to tell that this is science fiction? The references to unfamiliar details are the main clue – 'the fast food module', the 'leisure area', and the 'PREM'. Jan Mark combines familiar details with items that belong to a different world.

The best fantasy writing treats an unfamiliar world as if the reader already understands it. The writer presents it just as if she were writing about a railway station or country lane.

For example, in the hands of a less good writer, Jan Mark's story might read more like this:

> Arty squeezed past the home laundry unit. This was the maze of machines that automatically did the week's washing. He went past the fast food module, where food could be got at the touch of a control panel, and into the leisure area, where a range of electronic recreational items were available.

Notice how the interest of the text is spoilt because the reader is **told** everything by the writer: it loses its mystery, and it begins to feel more like an information text than a story.

To look at other features of fantasy and science fiction writing, compare Jan Mark's story with these extracts from a story in a different style by Leigh Brackett:

> The spaceship lay like a vast black whale, stranded on a spotless floe*. Behind it the icewall rose, its upper spires carved by the wind into delicate fantastic shapes…
>
> * floe – large block of ice, as found in the north and south Poles

Notice the way the writer uses a simile ('like a vast black whale') to help the reader to visualize something we have never seen.

Writing practice

Choose one of the following scenarios and try to write the opening of a story that feels very believable to the reader.

SEE ALSO: Writing strong story openings – page 102

Task A	An ice-castle built high in the mountains of a kingdom called Xeron. A white snow leopard guards the entrance as a stranger approaches… Describe the scene.

Task B	It is 2099. A child sits at home playing with toys. Most of them are quite different from the toys we know today. Describe the scene.

Building a storyline

Introduction

Alfred Hitchcock, a master of storytelling in film, once said: 'Drama is like real life with the dull bits cut out.' A good piece of fiction – novel or short story – should be the same. In a short story (which is what most storytelling in school is) your plot will probably fall into three main stages. How can you build these stages into a convincing, interesting storyline?

Getting started

Here is a very short story – just 55 words long.

> ### *First Encounter* by Arthur L Willard
>
> She had reservations. Lots of them. She thought the personal ads were for losers. But she was terribly lonely and maybe, just maybe…
> She placed the ad. The most promising answer arrived early. And now, here she was, waiting at the restaurant for a stranger with a rose in his lapel.
> 'Daddy? Is that you?'

Here are some possible structures to make it a longer story.

Story structure 1	Story structure 2	Story structure 3
Background to main character – who she is, where she lives, etc.	Main character in restaurant, worried, looking at watch.	Main character in restaurant, worried, regrets making this arrangement.
↓	↓	↓
She writes personal ad for local paper.	Gets out letter – we see what it says – arrangement to meet.	Flashback to writing ad.
↓	↓	↓
Week later – waiting for response.	Father walks in. Her reaction.	Cut back to restaurant – still no sign of 'date'.
↓		↓
Response arrives suggesting meeting at restaurant.		Flashback to reply to ad: we read it.
↓		↓
Waiting in restaurant – sees father walk in. Her reaction.		Cut back to restaurant – about to leave. Father arrives. Her reaction.

Notice:

- **Story structure 1** is the most straightforward way of telling the story – it starts at the beginning and continues step-by-step to the conclusion. It would be easy for the reader to follow. The first step – background description – could make it very slow to get started.
- **Story structure 2** begins more dramatically – we wonder why the woman is there. The letter shows us why. It's a simple but powerful three-step story.
- **Story structure 3** is more ambitious, using flashbacks to fill in information. The reader is quickly involved in the story, but the disjointed structure could confuse some readers.

Which structure do you think would work best?

Writing practice

52

As you can see, there is no single way of telling a story. Planning it out using stages, as above, can be a really good way of getting the overall structure right before you get down to writing the story in detail.

Practise building two storylines using this 55-word story. As above, aim to tell the story in two different ways:

SEE ALSO:
Making a chronological story interesting – page 94
Writing non-chronological stories – page 96
Writing strong story openings – page 102

> ### *A December Story* by Dean Christianson
>
> Nick DeSantos, mailman, scanned the dead letter bin. Hundreds of envelopes bore the same address: 'Santa Claus, North Pole'.
> 'Hate seeing disappointed kids,' Nick said to his supervisor.
>
> 'Serves 'em right,' he said. 'Believin' in Santa Claus.'
> Arriving home, Nick reached inside his bag and took out one of many letters.
> 'Dear Bobby,' Nick wrote.

Making a chronological story interesting

Introduction

From an early age we are taught that stories have a beginning, middle and end. Many of the stories we write ourselves use the same chronological structure – showing events in the order in which they happen.

But chronological stories can be dull. Because of their structure they can look like this:

Event 1 → Then Event 2 → Then Event 3 → And so on

The part that can become boring is the 'then', the way you move the storyline on. Here, for example, is how a young child would tell the story of a trip to the zoo:

> Harry got in the car and then he drove to the zoo and when he got there it was a really hot day. Then he bought his ticket and the first thing he saw was the monkeys. Then he went to the lions...

How would this be improved as a story?

It needs two ingredients:
- more detail about each event, so that as a reader we feel we are actually there, experiencing it (for more practice on this, see Section 9: Setting)
- a way of linking the events together that is more interesting than using 'and' and 'then'.

Getting started

Here are two different ways of linking events:

1 Using different discourse markers

Discourse markers tell a reader about the direction of a text, where the story or argument is heading. Discourse markers that are useful in writing narratives include:

**Later   Whilst   Once   After..., we...   Despite   Because
A while later**

Here is a new structure for the zoo story, using a bigger range of discourse markers. (The discourse markers have been highlighted.)

> **Event one:** Harry driving to the zoo.
> **Event two:** Once he had parked his car, Harry bought his ticket and went in...
> **Event three:** After spending ten minutes or so watching the monkeys, Harry moved on to find the lions...

Notice how the discourse markers:
- help move the story on
- add more variety to the story than simply saying 'and then'.

2   Cutting from scene to scene

The second way of making your narrative more interesting is to make the reader work harder. Instead of always using a discourse marker, you could just cut from one scene to another. This moves the story on in a very direct way – like this:

> End of event 1: ... So Harry turned into the zoo car park, found a space, and locked his car.
> Cut to event 2: The zoo reception was busy and Harry had to stand in line...
> Cut to event 3: Harry first noticed the noise the monkeys made. He watched them swinging between trees and ropes...

Notice:
- the pace of the story seems faster
- the style is closer to cinema and television – rapid cutting from one scene to the next
- it makes storytelling quicker because you don't have to link events so deliberately.

Writing practice

53

Using the two techniques here for making a chronological story interesting, take the story of Harry at the zoo and retell it for a young audience (5-8 year olds). Try to avoid linking events using 'and then'. Make up any details you need to about Harry and the zoo.
Remember your aim: to make the story interesting by linking events more creatively.

SEE ALSO:
Writing strong story openings – page 102
Writing powerful endings – page 104

Writing non-chronological stories

Introduction

Many of the stories we read in books and watch at the cinema and on television do not use a chronological structure: they avoid telling the story in the order in which it happened. Think of soap operas. The average scene in a soap lasts less than twenty seconds. Then we cut to another scene featuring different characters. Some novels do the same, cutting between storylines, or showing events which have already happened (flashbacks). These are techniques you might want to try in your own storytelling.

Getting started

Technique A: Telling more than one story at once

This technique is particularly popular in thrillers and detective stories. The writer introduces one character in one setting, and hooks our interest. Then we cut to another set of characters and another event. Then, perhaps, we cut back to the first scene, or to a third.

This opening to Minnette Walters' thriller *The Breaker* shows how she begins different sections – some very short – with a different focus:

> She drifted with the waves, falling off their rolling backs and waking to renewed agony every time salt water seared down her throat and into her stomach…
>
> The child sat cross-legged on the floor like a miniature statue of Buddha, the grey dawn light leeching her flesh of colour…
>
> Behind the questing mongrel which zigzagged energetically in pursuit of a scent, the horse picked its way carefully down the track that led from Hill Bottom to the Pool…
>
> The emergency services had rushed into action following a nine-nine-nine call to the police from a mobile telephone…

Notice:
- the reader has to work harder to make sense of the story – it gets us immediately involved
- the style raises questions in the reader's mind. Who are these people? Where are we? How is this scene linked to the last one?
- The writer changes style in different sections – some descriptive (a dog on a path), some more urgent (a 999 call).

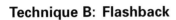

Technique B: Flashback

A flashback can **show** the reader something that happened earlier in a character's life, instead of the writer **telling** it.

> Mr Jones sat there, in the faded chair, biting his nails.
>
> A cat ran across the road and he knew he had to catch it. It would be his new pet, the first animal that belonged to him…

Notice:

- the sudden break in the narrative tells us that we have moved to a different time or place
- the use of the pronoun 'he' in the second sentence makes the reader guess who the character may be
- the technique allows the writer to give us background information about Mr Jones.

Writing practice

54

Take the story opening below and experiment with retelling it using the techniques in this unit: two different narratives and flashback.

> Kate is working late. She phones her partner Phil to tell him she will be delayed. They had a row this morning and she's happy not to rush home. But… it's Kate's birthday and Phil has arranged a surprise party. He has a house full of 40 guests. They're all sitting there waiting for Kate to return…

Tell the story using flashback to show the row this morning. Try to build in Phil's point of view as well. Your structure might be:

SEE ALSO: Exploring viewpoint – page 98

Kate at the office/phones Phil (from Kate's point of view)

↓

Flashback to this morning (from Kate's point of view)

↓

Meanwhile, Phil is planning a party (from Phil's point of view)

↓

Kate sets off home — discovers party (from Kate's point of view)

Exploring viewpoint

Introduction

When we tell stories, we have to decide whose point of view to use. The simplest decision is whether to use the first or third person mode – 'I' or 'she'/'he'.

First person mode:

> **As I was walking towards the shop, I noticed a small boy crying.**

Third person mode:

> **As she was walking towards the shop, Catherine noticed a small boy crying.**

It is also possible to use the second person mode, ('you') though it is fairly rare:

> **As you were walking towards the shop, you noticed a small boy crying.**

How do the different viewpoints create a different effect in the story?

Getting started

Take a simple story like this one:

> Boy called out of school assembly. No one knows why. They assume he's either in trouble or something has happened at home. Boy goes to Headteacher's office and is told that he has won a prize for his work in Drama. He returns to lessons pretending he's upset, just to show how good at Drama he is, before telling his friends the news.

Whose point of view could you tell this story from, and what would be the advantages of each?

The boy – first person	I'd only just arrived in assembly when I noticed Mrs Gull waving at me. I immediately wondered what I'd done, why I was in trouble.	**Effect:** This style feels most personal, most autobiographical. It allows us to see things through the eyes of the character and to feel what he is feeling.
The boy – third person	James had only just arrived in assembly when he noticed Mrs Gull waving at him. He immediately wondered what he'd done, why he was in trouble.	**Effect:** This allows good, clear storytelling, with the focus still on the main character. It allows the author to show other people's thoughts and feelings, too, because we are not confined to looking through the eyes of just one character.
The boy – second person	You had only just arrived in assembly when you noticed Mrs Gull waving at you. You immediately wondered what you'd done, why you were in trouble.	**Effect:** This style feels a bit odd, but can be powerful in some stories – for example, where one character is chasing or watching another. It can create a rather eerie effect with one person describing what someone else did. It feels a bit like a letter to the other person.

Notice all the other options you have:

Omniscient narrator (This gives the point of view of the author, rather than any single character. It is the way many of the early stories we hear are told.)	**Example:** The pupils were shuffling into assembly. Mr Foley watched them from the stage. At the back of the hall, a boy was about to whisper something to his friend, then changed his mind. Outside the rainclouds darkened.

Viewpoint of Mrs Gull (This shows us the event from the viewpoint of someone slightly involved.)	**Example:** As soon as the pupils were settled in assembly that morning, I thought I could sit back and relax. Assembly makes a tranquil start to the day. Then someone passed me a note. I can't even remember now who gave it to me, but on it were four words: James Auchincloss to Head.
Viewpoint of another pupil (This shows the viewpoint of someone who is a bystander – not directly involved.)	**Example:** We'd only just sat down in the hall. I was next to Sally and Mr Foley had just begun to speak. Then I noticed a slight commotion on my right. I looked across. Mrs Gull was bending down waving to catch James Auchincloss's eye. As usual he was in a world of his own. Someone giggled and then nudged him.
Viewpoint of Headteacher (Notice how this forces you to start the story from a different setting.)	**Example (first person):** I was hoping for a quiet time to open the post and make some telephone calls when the phone rang. Phone calls at this time are usually complaints from parents so I braced myself. This one carried good news – all about James Auchincloss. He had won a really high-powered Drama prize. James has had his share of problems recently, so I scrawled a note and asked my PA if she'd run it along to the Hall.

Notice that you still have more possibilities.
- You could use the Headteacher's viewpoint using third person mode ('Mrs Cameron had just settled into her office to try and get through the weekend's bag of post, when the telephone rang…')
- or a friend of James's
- or one of his parents.

And, of course, within a story, you might cut between different scenes. Each one might not only take place in a different setting, but show us the viewpoint of a different character.

Viewpoint, in other words, is one of the most powerful ways you have of adding interest, drama, or intrigue to your story.

Writing practice

55

Do some experiments with viewpoint. Take the storyline below and, as above, try telling the opening of the story from **three** or more different viewpoints. Use the guidelines below to help you.

Storyline:

> Sarah and Ray kicking a football about near their homes. Suddenly hear a car screech to a halt, then a lot of shouting. Man in car is shouting at girl saying she wasn't waiting in place they arranged. He seems to be her father. She's upset and embarrassed that he's telling her off. He says get into the car. She says no, she'll get the bus home instead. He drives off. Sarah and Ray go back to playing football.

SEE ALSO:
Writing strong story openings – page 102
Using dialogue to reveal character – page 84

Possible viewpoints:
- omniscient narrator (not showing us any single character's point of view)
- Ray or Sarah
- the girl
- the man in the car
- another bystander – a traffic warden, someone standing nearby
- the girl's mother (at home) hearing about it later.

Decide whether to use first, second or third person mode and see how the story changes as you shift the viewpoint.

Writing strong story openings

Introduction

Just as a newspaper or magazine journalist knows that the first sentence is vital to grab readers' attention, so the opening of a story is one of its most important features. The novelist Brian Moore used to rewrite his opening paragraphs up to 70 times until they felt right.

Writer Michael Baldwin says: 'An effective short story is one that hooks us with the first sentence and keeps us reading until the end.'

Getting started

According to Michael Baldwin, an opening sentence should contain one of three things:

1   An event

Something important is about to happen or is already happening. For example:

> *The first time I robbed Tiffany's it was raining.*
>
> John Cheever, *Montraldo*

> My father lost me to The Beast at cards.
>
> Angela Carter, *The Tiger's Bride*

2   A setting

We are introduced into a fascinating world. For example:

```
Inside the Maison Blondell the steam was so thick that
Mrs Watkins felt the tears gathering as she leaned over
the client's hand.
```

Roland Starke, *Lionel*

3   A starting idea

The opening is either so witty or strange that we feel we must read on. For example:

'MY MOTHER SAYS MY FATHER IS ON AN EXPEDITION UP THE AMAZON,' THE VERY SMALL BOY SAID. 'IF HE IS, THEN THE PIRANHAS MUST HAVE EATEN HIM,' HE ADDED AFTER A DECENT PAUSE.

Michael Baldwin, *Absent Fathers*

Notice:
- how these openings hint at who the character is and where the story is set
- that the openings sometimes use dialogue to introduce us to a character quickly
- how the writers choose their words carefully – there are no great slabs of description here.

Writing practice

56

Here are three fairly bad story openings – but they have some potential. Experiment with making them more interesting. You might:
- cut words
- retell them from a different viewpoint
- use dialogue
- rewrite them totally.

SEE ALSO: Writing powerful endings – page 104

The sea was really deep and I felt a bit afraid of walking further down the beach into it.

Mrs Newgate knew that something was wrong when she heard a rather strange sound that she hadn't heard before and worried what it might be, so she decided to go downstairs and investigate.

'I cannot tolerate this any longer,' said Todd and he walked out of the room in a huff.

Writing powerful endings

Introduction

With novels, we usually expect an ending which ties up many of the loose ends of the story. This does not have to mean a happy ending, but it will usually tell us what happens to the main characters.

Short stories are different. They are often designed to leave us surprised or disturbed at the end, or to leave a question unanswered.

Think of Roald Dahl's *Tales of the Unexpected*, which always feature a twist at the end that we didn't predict.

How can you write endings which will leave the reader surprised or laughing or impressed?

Getting started

This is probably the worst ending you could ever write:

> **… And at that moment I woke up and realized it had all been a dream.**

Why is it so awful? Because the reader feels that it's a letdown, a cheap way of finishing the story. All the tension immediately evaporates.

Here are some alternatives:

1 Open-ended endings

Leave the reader to work out what happens. Give a sentence which hints at what might have happened, or words which will stick in their memory for a few minutes. For example:

> **We looked again at the horizon. There was definitely something – just a speck – floating towards us.**

2 Dialogue

A character can say something which hints at what will happen in the future. For example:

> **'Okay,' she said. 'Maybe tomorrow.'**

3   Shock tactics

This is the Roald Dahl approach – giving a twist at the end of the story. For example:

> As he moved his hand finally to switch out the light, he realized in a sickening second that he was no longer alone. His old friend was back.

4   Description

Sometimes you can get a powerful effect by changing the focus away from your character to something in the setting. For example:

> 'No,' said Ralph. He looked away.
> A gust of wind lifted the branches and a scattering of red leaves fell slowly to the earth.

Writing practice

Take this story and practise writing different final paragraphs for it:

> A traveller listens to a barman's tale about a strange creature that lives out on the moors. The traveller goes out next day. Returns that night, agitated, and says to the barman that he didn't see anything. The barman knows he is lying and sees the bite marks on the back of his neck.

SEE ALSO: Writing strong story openings – page 102

It's a corny story – but see what different effects you can achieve by trying out the techniques listed above.

Building tension

Introduction

One of the reasons many of us enjoy reading stories is to find out what happens next. Building tension means keeping the reader waiting. It is a technique used a lot in thrillers and mysteries, in books, television, and movies. Careful timing is vital. You need to be able to keep the reader guessing, but not let the build-up go on so long that it becomes boring.

How can you build tension into your own stories?

Getting started

1   Sentence types

Short sentences, used carefully, can build tension. Their rhythm can create a feeling of worry and threat. Imagine this is the scene in your story:

> Amanda is walking home. It is just starting to get dark. She walks down a passageway and thinks she hears footsteps behind her.

Watch the effect of writing the story in two styles:

All longer sentences
Amanda set off home as it was starting to get dark. She felt the chill of the night air, so she cut through a passageway that ran between two newly-built houses. She ignored how dark the alley was and carried on walking, though she started to think she could hear footsteps behind her.

Longer sentences giving way to short sentences
Amanda set off home as it was starting to get dark. She felt the chill of the night air, so she cut through a small alleyway. When she stepped into it the darkness thickened. Amanda walked more quickly. What was that? She thought she'd heard something. She walked on. There it was again. Footsteps.

Notice:
- the second extract builds tension by showing us events from Amanda's viewpoint – we don't know any more than she does
- the short sentences make it feel disjointed, disturbing
- the details about the alleyway also build tension
- too many short sentences would become repetitive and boring – the secret is to vary your sentence style.

2   Atmospherics

You can build tension into a description by using emotive words (words carrying emotional associations) – such as 'darkness', 'fear', 'storm'. These words tend to create a feeling that all is not well. They are more powerful words than, say, 'street', 'road', 'alleyway', and can help to create a feeling of unease in the reader – like this:

> The darkness deepened. She looked for the end of the alley. Something was there, but not the light she was expecting. The wind lifted and the branches above her head began to scratch at the wooden fence beside her.

Notice how the choice of words creates a feeling of uneasiness. Be careful not to overdo it, though, because your writing will become corny and predictable.

3   Delaying action

When the reader wants to find out what will happen next, you can build tension by keeping her or him waiting. Cut to a one-sentence description of something instead. Focus on a sound or texture. Look how this device builds tension:

> Amanda peered harder into the gloom. A cat somewhere whined to be let in. Amanda's fists clenched tighter. There was someone there, she was sure. The wind tugged at the hood of her raincoat. She took a step further forward. A cloud drifted across the moon and the darkness thickened.

SEE ALSO:
Fitting characters into realistic settings – page 88
Creating fantasy settings – page 90
Choosing the right vocabulary – page 112

Notice:
* how the writing shifts from describing Amanda to other details
* how we are kept waiting to see what may be at the end of the passageway.

Writing practice

57

Take the scenario below and practise creating tension in it, using the three techniques outlined above.

> Boy on holiday with parents. Swims to small island not far from the beach he's been lying on. Briefly explores island. Comes back to see the tide has moved in fast. The island is going to be submerged and the crossing back to the beach is getting wider. He has to swim for it...

Getting the tense right

Introduction

Most stories are written in the past tense: they describe events that happened in the past. The openings of some traditional stories emphasize this:

> Once upon a time there was a man called Llewellyn who had a faithful hunting hound called Gelert…

> **A long time ago, in a galaxy far, far away…**

Most of the stories you read will use the past tense in a less obvious way:

> … I saw lots of her at school. She had no other friends. Nobody else could stand the embarrassment of pretending that they believed her awful lies.
>
> Anne Fine, *The Tulip Touch*

Tense is something we take for granted as we write stories, but it is something that can have a powerful impact on the overall effect of your writing.

Getting started

1 The past versus the present tense

The past tense is ideal for most stories because it describes events that have happened. To describe those same events in the present tense can seem odd and artificial. Here is an example:

A: Past tense	B: Present tense
I was walking through the supermarket when I saw Georgina from school. I decided to go and say hello. Strangely, she didn't seem pleased to see me. I could tell at once that something was wrong.	I am walking through the supermarket when I see Georgina from school. I decide to go and say hello. Strangely, she doesn't seem pleased to see me. I can tell at once that something is wrong.

Notice:
- Version A feels more straightforward – a piece of easy-to-follow storytelling
- Version B feels rather more like a diary. It works well for the emotional parts of the story ('I can tell at once that something is wrong') because it feels very immediate. But it seems a bit artificial for action ('I am walking through a supermarket').

2   The pluperfect tense

The pluperfect pushes events further back into the past by one stage. It can be really useful for showing the background to an event. Here is how it works:

> **Present tense**
> Greg hoped that the problems were over and that he could now enjoy a relaxing afternoon. He sat down to rest.

> **Pluperfect tense**
> Greg had hoped that the problems were over and that he would now be able to enjoy a relaxing afternoon. He had sat down to rest.

The pluperfect uses the verb forms 'had' and 'had been'. Look at how you can cut into the pluperfect to give a character some depth:

> Sophie stood by the bus stop, thinking. It had been years since the accident. She had hoped she would be able to forget it. Now it was back, haunting her.

In general though, you may want to avoid the pluperfect, except for special effects – because it can lead to ugly phrasing like 'she had had' and 'He would have had…'. Use it for sudden flashes into the past.

Writing practice

58

Take the story idea below and experiment with different tenses. Try writing part of it in the present tense to see what the effect is. Then write parts in the past tense, using the pluperfect to add information about the character's background.

SEE ALSO:
Choosing the right vocabulary – page 112
Using special techniques – page 114

> Stephen moves to new school. It's his first day and he's terrified. He thinks back to this time last week when he was at his last school – how much safer and more pleasant it had seemed.

Creating sentence variety

Introduction

We often assume that we read stories only to follow the characters and the storylines. But a writer's style can have an important influence upon us too. A tedious style is unlikely to make us want to read on, however interesting the characters or plot.

The key is to use a variety of sentences – otherwise your style can become uninteresting and even off-putting, as the examples below demonstrate.

Getting started

1 A rambling style: compound sentences

Some stories use a style based on compound sentences. These link lots of clauses together using conjunctions like 'and', 'but' and 'or'. This sentence style is the one we use mostly in speech – but notice how rambling it can seem if you use it too much in writing:

> Jessica was feeling unwell and decided to stay off work that day, but then she started to feel guilty and wondered what everyone at work might be thinking about her. She had been out with them all last night and they were probably saying that she had seemed fine and would be surprised that she wasn't at her desk today.

Notice:
- how breathless the style seems – we are desperate for greater control over the sentences
- how boring the style seems – and how longwinded
- how the use of 'and' and 'but' makes it feel like spoken language.

2 A disjointed style: simple sentences

Simple sentences contain one verb and tell us, usually, about one subject. As we saw on page 106, they can help to build tension in a story. But used too much at once, they can become repetitive and give a story a very disjointed feeling:

> Jessica was feeling unwell. She decided to stay at home. Then she began to feel guilty. She worried about the people at work. What would they think?

Notice:
- this style feels clearer than the mass of compound sentences above, but it also feels disjointed
- the short simple sentences give it a jerky tone
- we don't feel involved with Jessica – the style seems to get in the way.

3 A pompous style: complex sentences

Complex sentences use relative clauses ('the man, <u>whom I had seen earlier</u>, was back'), and adverbials ('however', 'despite', 'because') to link clauses together. They can add real polish to your writing – but too many at once creates a pompous style:

> Because she was unwell, Jessica decided to stay at home. Although she felt this was the right decision, she soon began to feel guilty. Her friends, who would know that she was not the kind of person to take time off, must still be wondering about her.

Notice:
- how pompous the style feels – more like a legal document than a story
- how the sentence structures become repetitive and boring.

Writing practice

Now look at the story told using a range of sentence styles. The variety gives it more interest. Based on what you have learnt in this unit, continue the story for another couple of paragraphs, experimenting with using a range of sentence styles.

SEE ALSO:
Getting the amount of description right – page 82
Using special techniques – page 114

Simple sentence kicks the story off and grabs our attention.

> Jessica was feeling unwell. Despite being fine last night, this morning she felt terrible. She decided that she had to stay at home, but then started wondering about her decision...

Complex sentence moves the story on; changes the rhythm.

Compound sentence tells us more about what Jessica does.

Choosing the right vocabulary

Introduction

Just as getting your sentence style right is important to the effect of your story, so is choosing the right vocabulary. Film makers can tell their stories through pictures, letting their audience see characters and settings for themselves. As a writer your role is different: you use words to create the pictures in the reader's mind.

Here are some guidelines on choosing the right words.

Getting started

1   Choose words which are visual

Try to help your reader see the scene you are describing. Describe locations, weather, textures, colours – but without overdoing it.

Look at this example:

> Mrs Price stood in her drawing-room in the bright afternoon sunshine waiting for the funeral guests to come in from the churchyard at the end of the garden. They were at present in groups under the lych-gate, quiet and well turned-out like their cars, which were standing about the drive and the leafy lane beyond.
>
> Jane Gardam, *The Summer After the Funeral*

Notice:
- how vivid the description is
- the powerful, visual words and phrases – 'bright afternoon sunshine', 'well turned-out'
- how they hook our interest and make the scene seem real.

2   Avoid overwriting

There is always a big temptation to overwrite – either by using fancy words from a thesaurus, or by piling up too many adjectives and adverbs. Look at how the power of the text is reduced if you do this.

a) Using long words where short ones will do:

> Mrs Price was stationed in her drawing-room in the effulgent postmeridian sunshine waiting for the funeral invitees to enter from the necropolis at the boundary of the garden.

Notice:
- how awful this is – no one would want to keep on reading it
- how the power of the original description has been lost by using fancy vocabulary.

b) Using adjectives and adverbs for their own sake:

> Old Mrs Price stood in her majestically faded drawing-room in the bright afternoon sunshine waiting patiently for the grim-faced funeral guests to come slowly in from the cramped churchyard at the end of the magnificent garden.

Notice how we lose the impact of the story – we have to wade through all the description. The adjectives and adverbs get in the way.

3   Be self-critical

No one can give you cast-iron advice on vocabulary. You have to decide for yourself which word works best in its context. When in doubt, cut a word out. Whenever possible, see if you can think of a better word – but not one which you only know from a thesaurus.

Writing practice

59

Look at this terrible story opening. There are certainly problems with the vocabulary. What changes would you make? Rewrite the story so that the choice of vocabulary is more successful:

SEE ALSO: Writing strong story openings – page 102

> The sun, a huge golden globe, beat down from amid an azure sky. On the crowded beach below, a frenetic blaze of activity was taking place with people running madly around, playing giddy games, diving bravely into the clear blue attractive seas of the beautiful bay. Shane sat confidently astride his newly-purchased lilo, which bobbed gently upon the lapping waves of the salty sea. He felt the sun's rays biting into his pink shoulders and realized immediately that he should have applied more lavishly a layer of suntan cream. Too late, he thought introspectively, and pulled on the plastic goggles he had persuaded his parents to purchase for him earlier that day at the corner shop which was piled high with various items for tourists and holidaymakers.

Using special techniques

Introduction

Fiction writers sometimes use three special techniques to make their writing more powerful:

- Similes
- Metaphors
- Personification

Used with care (i.e. not too often) you will find that they can improve the quality of your storytelling, too.

Getting started

1   Similes

Similes work by comparing one thing to another.

Imagine you want to make a stranger seem menacing. You could say: 'The stranger was menacing'; or you could use a simile to help create that impression:

> **The stranger appeared on the dusty path like a serpent.**

> **The man stood there, as still as night.**

> **The man spoke, his voice like a dog's growl.**

In your own writing you might use similes to show:
- what something looks like
- how it moves
- the weather.

2   Metaphors

Metaphors are comparisons, like similes, but they are less obvious. They do not use 'like' or 'as' to signal that something is being compared to something else.

We use metaphors in everyday language. Take the topic of battle:

> **She attacked his views. He defended himself. I won the argument.**

Metaphors can have a powerful effect in your writing, helping the reader to see a character or scene more strongly:

> **Metaphor: He walked in, a stranger to her.**
> (Simile: He walked in like a stranger to her.)
> **Metaphor: A tide of nausea swept over me and I ran out of the room.**
> (Simile: Nausea swept over me like a tide...)
> **Metaphor: The room exploded with light.**
> (Simile: The sudden flood of light in the room was like an explosion.)

3 Personification

This technique takes things that are not alive (the weather, objects, concepts) and describes them as if they were. It can be a powerful way of creating fear, or bringing a situation more fully to life.

> **The clouds galloped across the sky. (Clouds compared to horses.)**
>
> **Wind scratched the door, trying to get in. (Wind compared to an unwelcome stranger.)**
>
> **Death stalked the village, seeking its next victim. (Death compared to a murderer.)**

Writing practice

Take the scenario below and practise writing sentences which use the techniques of simile, metaphor, and personification. In your own story, you would not want to use all three techniques so much – that would lead to a very flowery, off-putting style. This is an opportunity to experiment with the techniques so that you can then build them into your own work when appropriate.

SEE ALSO: Using description to reveal more about a character – page 80 Getting the amount of description right – page 82

Scenario: a storm is brewing. Someone is rushing to get home, pushing a bike where the chain has obviously broken. The storm is menacing and the person looks worried.

Bring the scene to life using simile, metaphor and personification.

Style features of different genres

Introduction

Probably without even realizing it, you are able to recognize types of stories – genres (like war stories, westerns, fantasy, horror, romance, etc.) – by their written styles. This is a useful skill which will help you in writing your own stories. Each genre uses its own ranges of vocabulary and grammar, and a particular tone.

Getting started

Use these story extracts to examine the style features of three different genres:

a In the morning I saddled the grey and rode into town, not hurrying because I didn't like what I was going to do. But I had thought this all out after the trail was over, and I couldn't see any other answer that would let me sleep at night.

Jack Schaefer, *Miley Bennett*

Genre: Western

Vocabulary: informal, assuming the reader is familiar with words like 'grey'. Concrete words rather than abstract concepts (e.g. 'grey', 'town', 'trail')

Grammar: chiefly compound sentences (clauses linked by 'and' and 'but') giving a conversational feel

Tone: feels like someone telling us a story – in other words, autobiographical. But there is a hint of menace too: 'I didn't like what I was going to do.' Despite the casual surface, this writer's work builds tension from the first sentence.

b Once upon a time there was a young man who went out into the world to seek his fortune with nothing but a pleasant face, good health and a kind heart.

Diana Ross, *The Young Man with Music in his Fingers*

Genre: fairy tale

Vocabulary: simple, abstract words – 'young', 'world', 'fortune', 'health'

Grammar: complex sentence using the familiar phrasing of fairy tales – in particular, 'Once upon a time'

Tone: simple, neutral tone

> **C** Moments before, as the six of them, a sergeant and five class privates, had crawled over the desert sand, a Nazi machine gunner had spotted them, and had cut loose. And the six of them, as one, had taken a running dive head-first into a shallow bomb crater and burrowed like gophers into the hot sand.
>
> Chester Himes, *Two Soldiers*

Genre: war story

Vocabulary: specialized, technical ('class privates', 'cut loose'); specific about places ('desert sand', 'bomb crater'); not much description – emphasis on action

Grammar: complex, lots of detail in long sentences to create a feeling of confusion

Tone: urgent, full of action. Simile 'like gophers' emphasizes the way the soldiers are having to flee like animals.

Writing practice

60

Experiment with genres by writing the opening paragraphs of these stories using the framework below:

Character: Frank Rogers, aged 47

Genre 1: war story: Frank Rogers is sheltering with his troops in a hut.

Genre 2: science fiction: Frank Rogers gets home from work. Automated systems welcome him back, prepare his meal, etc.

Genre 3: horror: Frank Rogers finds himself in a large crate. A hatch opens and a tarantula is pushed inside.

Genre 4: romance: Frank Rogers starts work at a new office where the boss – Stacey Quinton – seems to be deliberately ignoring him.

Genre 5: spy story: Frank Rogers hovers at the edge of a street in a European city watching a man sipping coffee at a street café.

SEE ALSO: Making places seem real – page 86 Fitting characters into realistic settings – page 88 Creating fantasy settings – page 90 Building tension – page 106

Learning about the KS3 tests

Introduction

In early May in Year 9 you will sit the national tests in English. Your English teacher will give you more details about what will be required. This unit tells you more about the format and expectations of the tests. The next unit gives you advice and practice in how to approach the activities.

Format of the paper

Here is what you need to know about the writing paper:

Reading task
- You have 15 minutes reading time to read two passages – one fiction, one non-fiction.
- Then you answer three questions on the two passages.

Writing task
The Writing section gives you three options. You choose just **one** of the tasks. The tasks often include:
- one non-fiction writing activity (letter, eye-witness account, speech, article)
- one fiction writing activity ('Write the start of a story…'; 'Write an account or description…')

These tasks are related to the reading you have done earlier on the paper.

For example, in the 1999 paper students read an article about the Loch Ness monster. They then had to choose **one** of these writing tasks:

a) Imagine you saw, or thought you saw, the Loch Ness Monster.
Write an eye-witness account of the experience, making it as convincing and detailed as possible.

OR

b) Write a letter to a friend about an unusual event, explaining your thoughts and feelings about what happened.
You could write about a real or made-up event.
    You could begin:
    Dear…
    You are the only person who might believe what I am about to tell you…

    For this answer, you do not need to put an address at the top of the letter, but you should end it appropriately.

OR

c) Write an article for a travel magazine, describing a place that is beautiful but mysterious.

In your writing you could:

    Try to create the atmosphere of the place in your description;

    Aim to persuade readers that this place would be an interesting place to visit.

Notice:

- that you have a choice of which question you choose – you only do one of the tasks
- the phrasing of each task usually tells you which **genre** you are expected to write in – eyewitness account, letter, article
- the questions often provide further advice underneath the main question: this can give you helpful clues about how to structure your answer.

You should aim to spend 35 minutes on the question, leaving yourself five minutes to check through your whole paper.

You are assessed on:

- your ideas, organization and expression
- your ability to write clearly, using paragraphs and accurate grammar, spelling and punctuation.

Writing practice

Which of the activities on this paper would **you** choose to do?

How would you approach the task? What would be the first thing you write down?

How to write well in the KS3 tests

Introduction

The last unit showed you what kind of writing tasks you could meet in the KS3 tests. Now explore ways of writing well in test conditions.

Imagine that this written task follows a reading passage which argues that schools should involve local people more.

> Write a letter to your Headteacher suggesting ways of getting the community more involved in your school.
>
> You might discuss:
> * lessons during the school day to which visitors could contribute
> * other activities in which local people could be involved
>
> You do not need to put an address at the top of the letter, but you should end it appropriately.

Getting started

Step 1: Brainstorm (5 minutes)

1 Re-read the question. Look at the bullet-points. You must make sure you cover the points here.
2 Write down as many ideas as you can about adult visitors being involved in lessons – which lessons? What would the visitors do? What role would they take? How would they benefit? How would the students, staff and school as a whole gain?
3 Write down ideas for community use of the school at other times – before school, at lunchtimes, after school, at weekends, during holidays. Are there sporting facilities, computers, conference facilities? What role could students play?

Step 2: Structuring your ideas (1 minute)

1 Take your ideas and organize them into four or five main topics. This will help you to ensure that you use paragraphs (vital for getting a good result). Your structure might look like this:

> 1 – ways of involving the community in lessons
> 2 – benefits
> 3 – ways of extending community use of the school at other times
> 4 – benefits

2 As you write, tick these points off one by one, so that you're certain of writing in a clearly-structured way.

Step 3: Writing (30 minutes)

1 Remember the genre: this is a letter. Remind yourself of how to lay out a formal letter. Write the date and the addressee's name.

2 Think about the tone: the audience (your Headteacher) requires using a formal tone. Keep the vocabulary formal. Avoid elisions (say 'is not' rather than 'isn't').

3 Start paragraphs with a topic sentence so that it is clear to the examiner what your topic is.

4 Try to back up points with specific examples, so that your writing isn't all general opinions.

5 Aim to use a variety of sentences, to keep your style interesting.

6 Conclude formally: 'Yours sincerely', then your name.

Step 4: Checking (4 minutes)

Read through all your writing, on the whole paper. Read critically, making any necessary corrections.

Writing practice

Of course, this process looks easy on paper, but it also works in practice. You just need some time practising in timed conditions.

Use these questions to practise the brainstorming and planning process:

Fiction task	Write the opening to a story about two friends who fall out with each other. You might start by showing: • where the story takes place; and • who the two friends are.	Non-fiction task	Write an article for a local newspaper saying why people should have faith in the younger generation, rather than criticizing them all the time. In your writing you could: • give examples of positive activities done by young people • refer to the negative way young people are often portrayed in the media.

Extended assignments

Introduction

The extended assignments are designed to let you practise your writing skills in a series of genres and over a number of lessons and homeworks. By the end, you will have built up a collection of writing tasks ready for assessment by your teacher.

Each extended assignment includes writing in a variety of genres. Remember to look back to the appropriate unit to remind yourself of the style and format of each one.

For all of the writing activities, photocopiable writing frames are provided in the Writing Frames book.

Extended assignment A

Strange sightings

Context:
Alex Peterson is a reporter on a local newspaper. He receives a phone call one afternoon asking him to meet an unnamed person at nightfall at the edge of a field in the middle of nowhere. It is a meeting that will have a deep effect…

Activity 1: Notes

Alex finds the spot – a field next to a wood. 100 metres away the lights of a local pub shine out. In the field is a menacing scarecrow. Then Alex encounters a strange old man in dark glasses and a cap. He says: 'Be here tomorrow night and you'll see a sight that will make your fortune.' Then he slips off into the bushes and disappears. Alex looks around, making a few notes and sketches.

Write the entry in his notebook, including a sketch of the large field, describing Alex's impressions of:
• the old man
• the field
• what might happen tomorrow.

Activity 2: Diary

Alex has a sleepless night plagued with odd dreams. Next day is bright and clear. Alex works at the office and then, as told, heads to the mysterious field. A small group of people are there with binoculars. All of them keep themselves to themselves. The sky is dark and getting cloudy. Then – from behind a cloud – there's something like lightning, plus a humming sound. The sky begins to light up and something – a helicopter? – sinks into the field. The locals all crouch behind hedges. Alex takes a photograph. The machine in the field is huge and noisy. It does nothing but sit there. Just as suddenly as it arrived, it leaves, floating up into the clouds and disappearing.

Alex is astonished and drives home along country lanes in a daze.

Write Alex's diary for that evening, describing:
• the sights and sounds in the field
• Alex's emotions then and now.

Activity 3: Email

Next day Alex arrives early at work and logs on to the computer system. There is an email message waiting. It is a warning not to get involved in the events of last night and not to write about them. It is not clear who the message is from.

Write the email message.

Activity 4: Report

Alex visits the local library and looks up the site of the strange visit. Gradually, piecing together different records, it emerges that there have been strange sightings there throughout the past 80 years.

Write one eyewitness account written in the past. (To make it look like an old document you might use paper soaked in tea or coffee and burned around the edges.)

Activity 5: Letter

Alex is uncertain what to do next. It is clear that this is a major story. But there is also that threatening email to think about. Alex writes to a friend asking advice.

Write an informal letter:
• saying what has happened so far
• asking what to do next.

Extended assignments continued

Activity 6: Article

Alex's friend says it is important to reveal the truth of what has happened and that Alex has done nothing wrong. So Alex writes a front page exclusive describing:
- the events of the other evening
- the history that has been revealed.

Write the article, including the headline.

Extended assignment B

A summer murder mystery

Context:
You are staying at a small seaside hotel in the resort of Aldwold. There are around 13 other guests.

Activity 1: Diary

You arrive in Aldwold around 3pm after a long drive from home. You check into the hotel, and look at your slightly shabby room overlooking the hotel garden. You notice some of the other guests in the lounge – an elderly woman reading; two young men playing snooker; a businessman in the garden speaking quietly into a mobile phone. You take a walk along the sea front to get some air.

Write your diary entry for this first day.

August 17

Activity 2: Letter

Dinner in the hotel restaurant is a lively affair. You see other guests, and sit at a table with the businessman and the elderly woman. He drinks too much and becomes embarrassing.

Next morning a letter has been pushed under your door. It starts off pleasantly and then tells you you should leave the hotel at once for your own safety.

Write the letter. It begins:

> Dear Resident,
> I don't know your name and I hope you're
> enjoying your holiday.

Activity 3: Report

You worry about the note and show it to the hotel manageress. She refuses to discuss it, saying simply, 'There are lots of cranks around.' You take the note to the local police station. A police officer interviews you and then writes a report about:
- who you are
- the letter you received

Write the report. Set it out like this:

> Aldwold Police HQ
> Interview Report
> Date:
> Interviewee:

Activity 4: Brochure

You decide to spend the day away from the hotel. You pick up some brochures at the local tourist information centre. One is all about Aldwold.

Put together one page of the brochure, telling people about the charms of this old-fashioned seaside resort.

Activity 5: Informal letter

You return at teatime to the hotel. It is filled with activity. The businessman is lying on the floor and everyone is waiting for an ambulance to arrive. A local doctor is on the scene and says she thinks the businessman has been poisoned. Terrified, you retreat to your room. Another note is waiting under your door. This one tells you that you must get out tonight. This is enough. You decide it's time to leave. Before you go, you write a hasty letter to a best friend describing the events that have taken place and why you have decided to leave.

Write the letter.

Activity 6: Story

It is one year later. You are on holiday with friends in Ibiza. You have forgotten last year's strange couple of days in Aldwold. Lying on the beach, you reach into your bag and pull out the novel you've chosen to read on holiday. You open the inside cover. The picture of an elderly woman there looks familiar – but you can't quite place her. Then you begin to read. The plot feels very familiar. It's the events of the hotel last year – with you yourself as a minor character.

Write the opening chapter of the novel based on the events in the hotel.

Extended assignment C

Tourism project

Context:
Your local town or village is aiming to attract more tourists into the area. Schools have been asked to think of ways that they can also be involved.

Activity 1: Formal letter

Write a letter from the Chief Executive of your local council to your Headteacher saying:
• what the council is aiming to achieve (increased income from tourism, publicizing places of interest and facilities, and so on)
• how schools can help.

Activity 2: Speech

Your Headteacher decides to open this event up to students. S/he uses an assembly to explain what the council is asking, and to ask for any suggestions from students about:
• ways of improving the image of the school
• ways of encouraging tourists to use its facilities.

Write the speech.

Activity 3: Report

You are asked to draw up a small report showing what facilities your school could offer and what still needs to be developed. Write a report (one side of A4) for your Headteacher.

Activity 4: Leaflet

Publicity for the school will be vital. You are asked to produce a brochure telling tourists about your school's facilities, and persuading them to come and use them during the holidays.

Activity 5: Letter

You are a parent who objects to the use of the school. You feel it is there for the use of students, not tourists. Imagine the letter you might write to the local newspaper complaining about this policy of the local council.

Activity 6: Diary

Imagine a child on holiday has been to visit your school and has used some of the facilities. Write an entry in her/his diary saying what she did.

Acknowledgements

We are grateful to the following for permission to reprint copyright material:

Curtis Brown Ltd, London, on behalf of Mrs Susan Wells for extract from Susan Hill: *Mrs De Winter* (Sinclair Stevenson, 1993), copyright © Susan Hill 1993; Express Syndication for extract from report 'A school Sports Day was ruined...', Daily Star, 20.7.99; John Hamm, speech writer, on behalf of Sue Suter for extracts from 'Women with Disabilities: How to Become a Boat Rocker in Life', *Gifts of Speech*, http://gos.sbc.edu; Independent Newspapers (UK) Ltd for extract from Andrew Marshall: 'The man on the moon', *The Independent*, 17.7.99; and for headline and opening of article 'Grants and loans chaos looms for all students', *Independent on Sunday*, 25.7.99, both copyright © Independent Newspapers, 1999; Alfred A Knopf, a dvision of Random House, Inc for extract from Richard Schickel: *Clint Eastwood: A Biography* (Knopf, 1996); Mirror Syndication International for headline and opening of article 'Criminal', *The Sunday Mirror*, 25.7.99; and headline and opening of article 'She's my double miracle', *The Sunday People*, 25.7.99; Geoff Muench of Geoff's Bike Hire for extract from leaflet 'Guided Cycle Tours of Cambridge'; News International Syndication for headline and opening of article 'Mortgage bosses face police probe', *The Sunday Times*, 25.7.99, copyright © News International Newspapers Ltd, 1999; Running Press, Philadelphia and London for 'First Encounter' by Arthur L Willard and 'A December Story' by Dean Christianson, from *The World's Shortest Stories* edited by Steve Moss, copyright © 1998, 1995 by Steve Moss (Running Press, 1995); and to QCA Enterprises Ltd for permission to reproduce sample questions from National Tests at KS3 in English, 1999.

We have tried to trace and contact all copyright holders before publication. If notified the publishers will be pleased to rectify any errors or omissions at the earliest opportunity.

The publishers would like to thank the following for permission to reproduce photographs:

Corbis UK Ltd: p 63; Corbis UK Ltd/Chris Hellier: p 20/23; Corbis UK Ltd/John-Marshall Mantel: p 36; Corbis UK Ltd/Roger Tidman: p 29; Corel Professional Photos: pp 55, 66, 93; Oxford University Press: p 10; Stockbyte: p 43.

Artwork on page 71 is by Amanda Wood

Cover image: Tony Stone Images / Kevin Irby